GOD DWELLS WITH HIS PEOPLE

GOD DWELLS WITH HIS PEOPLE

A Study of Israel's Ancient Tabernacle

PAUL M. ZEHR

Introduction by
Myron S. Augsburger

HERALD PRESS
Scottdale, Pennsylvania
Waterloo, Ontario

Library of Congress Cataloging-in-Publication Data

Zehr, Paul M. 1936-
God dwells with his people.

Bibliography: p.
Includes index.
1. Tabernacle. 2. Jesus Christ—Person and offices. I. Title.
BM654.Z43 1981 296.6'5 80-22701
ISBN 0-8361-1939-8 (pbk.)

The paper in this publication is recycled and meets the minimum requirements of American National Standard for Information Sciences—Permanence of Paper for Printed Library Materials, ANSI Z39.48-1984.

Cover photograph and inside photographs by Jonathan Charles (except photographs for figures 6, 16, and 17 by Everett Newswanger).

GOD DWELLS WITH HIS PEOPLE

Library of Congress Catalog Card Number: 80-22701
International Standard Book Number: 0-8361-1939-8
Printed in the United States of America
Design by Alice Shetler

07 06 05 04 03 02 01 00 99 10 9 8 7 6

To order or request information, please call
1-800-759-4447 (individuals); 1-800-245-7894 (trade).
Website: www.mph.org

To my wife,
Mary.

CONTENTS

LIST OF FIGURES

AUTHOR'S PREFACE

For the past decade I have been involved in a tourist ministry directly related to the tabernacle described in the Book of Exodus. Many of these years were spent at the tabernacle replica in St. Petersburg, Florida, and the remainder of the time with the tabernacle reproduction in Lancaster, Pennsylvania.

Through this experience of study and lecturing to literally thousands of tourists, I have been exposed to a multitude of concepts and ideas on the ancient tabernacle and its interpretation. I vividly recall one visitor who, after looking at the ark of the covenant, asked, "Is this Noah's ark?" I have also met, on the other hand, many persons (both Hebrew and Christian) who have studied the tabernacle at length and freely offered helpful ideas on its construction and meaning. I owe much to them.

Out of this dialogue with thousands of persons, I have keenly felt the need for writing a book that clarifies the subject. I am well aware that many have taken pen in hand and published books about this ancient structure. Why then should I add to the many books that already are available to the reader?

My answer to that question is threefold. First, the tabernacle leads one into Israel's experience with God at Mt. Sinai where the covenant was established and Israel became God's covenant people. It is my belief that the plagues, Passover, Exodus, and the Sinai setting with the covenant, tabernacle, and law is the very heart of the Old Testament. The tabernacle itself takes one to the very heart of Israel's worship of God as a covenant people.

Second, one cannot fully understand the New Testament teaching regarding redemption nor the church as a covenant community without some knowledge of Israel's life and its tie to the ancient tabernacle. The New Testament explanation of the church draws upon more ideas from the tabernacle than from the temple. As a matter of fact, the Solomonic temple receives very little attention in the minds of the New Testament writers when compared with the amount of thought given to the ancient tabernacle. For example, notice the tabernacle imagery in these passages:

> You know that you were ransomed from the futile ways inherited from your fathers, not with perishable things such as silver or gold, but with the precious blood of Christ, like that of a lamb without blemish or spot. 1 Peter 1:18, 19.

> Our fathers had the tent of witness in the wilderness, even as he who spoke to Moses directed him to make it, according to the pattern that he had seen. . . . Yet the Most High does not dwell in houses made with hands; as the prophet says,
> "Heaven is my throne,
> and earth my footstool. . . ." Acts 7:44, 48.

Notice how Peter describes the church as a new covenant community in the language of Exodus 19.

> But you are a chosen race, a royal priesthood, a holy nation, God's own people, that you may declare the wonderful deeds of

> him who called you out of darkness into his marvelous light. Once you were no people but now you are God's people; once you had not received mercy but now you have received mercy. 1 Peter 2:9, 10.

Third, many of the books available on the tabernacle have a tendency to go to extreme either in their interpretation of its types and symbols or do not go far enough. Those that go to extreme in typology often fail to grasp the meaning of the tabernacle for Israel in its historical setting. And those that do not go far enough fail in picking up the New Testament interpretation of the tabernacle.

It is hoped that the following pages will present a balanced view.

I owe a word of gratitude to the Lancaster Conference of the Mennonite Church for allowing me extra time for research in preparation to set up the tabernacle reproduction for the tourists who visit the Lancaster County area. Without that extra research I could not have supervised the building of the reproduction of the Hebrew tabernacle, nor could I have written these pages. I want to thank the many tourists who have added their word here and there throughout these past ten years.

I also express my appreciation to Paul M. Lederach who gave valuable information regarding organization of the material and style of writing. And finally, I owe much to my wife, Mary, and our four children who have given up happy family time in order that this book could be completed.

Paul M. Zehr
Lancaster, Pennsylvania

INTRODUCTION

The history of the Bible is His story. It is God who is sovereign, who acts to reveal Himself, and who acts to redeem man. We refer to salvation history as an affirmation of faith that God has acted in history in grace, that He has moved to us in redemption.

Recognizing progress of doctrine, it can be said that compassing both Testaments is one covenant of grace. God acts in history to create a people for Himself, a people with whom He identifies. This study of the tabernacle sets forth this word, that God dwells with His people. The author, Paul Zehr, shows the development of this consciousness of God's presence, from the tabernacle worship to the incarnation and to the gift of the Holy Spirit from the risen Christ. To say that God works in history is not enough, there must be those who have the faith to interpret.

The study of the Old Testament has relevance for God's people today for numerous reasons: (1) the historicity of God's saving acts; (2) the unfolding of revelation culminating in Christ; (3) the character of the covenant community; (4) the reaction of faith to failure; (5) theological reflection on the problems of evil and of suffering; (6) discernment of God's purposes for the nations; (7) theological issues in comparative religions; (8) attitudes toward the orders and rites of religion; (9) understanding God's purposes for the future; and (10) the manner in which the people of God have read and used sacred literature.

This study of the Tabernacle is an effective work, in which the author relates the Old Testament to the New in a careful and scholarly way. He avoids extremes and analogies which would do violence to the historical setting of the accounts while he applies New Testament insights to Old Testament types. The emphasis upon God's covenant people, upon God in grace identifying with the people He is redeeming, relates the Tabernacle consistently to the central theme of the totality of the Old Testament Scripture. The reader may readily pursue this theme throughout the Old Testament, finding the key to difficult passages in the prophets as well. For example, this is true in Ezekiel 9 and 11, where in judgment upon Israel's sin the glory of God's presence is described as departing from the temple, and then from the city of Jerusalem. And further, it is evident in the New Testament where Jesus is called "Immanuel, God with us," and again in reference to the presence of the Spirit of God when we are told that our bodies are the temple of the Holy Spirit.

The author accepts the historicity of the Tabernacle in the wilderness, as do all conservative biblical scholars, while at the same time giving evidence of understanding form criticism and the documentary hypothesis. Accepting the historical creation of the Tabernacle at Sinai, even though the traditions may not have been put into their present written form until exilic or postexilic time, the author effectively sets worship at the center of Israel's life from the earliest period of their peoplehood. This book is an excellent guide in Old Testament study. Its uniqueness lies in the careful way in which the author relates the Old and New Testaments, focusing the greater meaning on redemption in Christ, and on the new covenant community.

My personal association with the project of the Tabernacle replica with which Zehr has worked, and my acquaintance and friendship with the author through the years adds to my appreciation of this work. I commend the author for sharing this meaningful study, and recommend the careful reading of this volume with confidence in the integrity of his interpretation. Let it guide us in the worship of God that will seek Him in longing and long for Him in seeking, that will find Him in loving and love Him in finding.

Myron S. Augsburger
Princeton, New Jersey

GOD DWELLS WITH HIS PEOPLE

1
SETTING AND COURTYARD

The Judeo-Christian tradition is one of the great religious movements in history. Western civilization continues to be shaped by its monotheistic and ethical principles. Through dispersion, migration, and missionary efforts Christians now span the globe. Jewish people likewise are found throughout the world.

Many common beliefs tie Christians and Jews together. Both affirm God's revelation of Himself and His will for humanity. Both agree that the Old Testament is God's revelation to mankind, a special book about God and His people. Christians need to discover anew their indebtedness to ancient Israel and the Old Testament. Perhaps the Jewish community needs to discover that Christianity is not opposed to Judaism but rather brings Judaism to its fulfillment and completion in the full revelation of God and His will for mankind in the New Testament. One way these concepts find expression is through a study of the ancient tabernacle described in the Old Testament, used by Moses, Aaron, and the children of Israel, and interpreted by the New Testament writers.

The tabernacle consisted of a courtyard with a brazen altar and laver placed in the east half. The main tabernacle building with its holy place and most holy place stood in the west half of the courtyard. The courtyard itself was set apart from Israel's encampment by a fence.

There are two major narratives on the tabernacle in the Book of Exodus; chapters 25-31 and chapters 35-40. Though minor differences exist between the narratives, the basic material is not in conflict.[1] The primary emphasis in these narratives in Exodus is the movement from God to man. They begin with a description of the ark of the covenant and the most holy place and then move outward to the courtyard and the encampment of the tribes.

While there is merit in moving from God to man, especially in a study of the scheme of divine revelation, the reader is better able to discover its meaning in the scheme of divine redemption by beginning with man in the encampment and moving inward toward the most holy place and God's presence at the ark of the covenant. This book will follow the latter approach although it does not limit itself to divine redemption.

One finds difficulty in understanding the tabernacle by merely plunging into the tabernacle narratives. We need to reach back into the wider setting of Israel as a covenant people related to God in order to begin to grasp the meaning of the tabernacle and its place in Israel's worship of God.

The Setting

Abraham's call (Genesis 12:1-3) marks, for all practical purposes, the beginning of the Hebrew people and the concept of the people of God. In her earliest period Israel was a people living under God's care. Hebrew religion did not have a humanistic origin. Unlike the other religions which sought after a god or gods, the Hebrew religion was solidly based on God coming to man. *Abraham was called of God.*

And this divine election had as its purpose the creating of a people of God.

Nationhood was not to be confused with politics. Israel's understanding of herself as God's people was quite different from the modern state of Israel. In fact, the high point of Israel's life in the Old Testament seems not to have been the so-called Kingdom period (c. 1000 BC to 587 BC). When Israel began to live like her pagan neighbors with a human king and thinking of their peoplehood in terms of political and geographical boundaries, then trouble came. It is clear that Israel's creative and dynamic period of spiritual life came before the so-called golden age of Solomon's empire by the way the prophets called the people back to the law and the covenant.

With the call of Abraham came the covenant. A covenant is an agreement between two or more parties. But the biblical concept of *berith*, or covenant, is more than an agreement. It is an act of God in which He comes to man and offers man various promises within that covenant relationship if man will respond in agreement to the terms of the covenant. In short, the covenant agreement between God and His people implies relationship which is the very heart of religion. God's covenant with Abraham formed the basis from which later covenants arose, including the final, climactic covenant agreement between God and man in Jesus Christ. The Sinaitic covenant, given years later, did not annul the covenant with Abraham. It was one major step in carrying forth the intent of the Abrahamic covenant. Any serious study of the tabernacle, therefore, must be seen against the background of the developing covenantal relationship between God and His people that finds its beginning with Abraham and its grand climax in the covenant in Jesus Christ.

Out of Egypt

When the Book of Exodus opens, we find the children of Israel in Egypt suffering in slavery. Sociologically, Israel already functioned as a people of God before the Exodus. Moses was called to become Israel's leader. Not only did he lead the people out of Egypt, but also he became Israel's greatest spiritual leader. During the Mosaic period Israel's spiritual life greatly developed as a monotheistic religion with Yahweh as its God.* The tabernacle with its cloud of glory representing the divine presence, constantly reminded Israel of the God who brought them out of Egypt.

One dynamic feature of Israel's monotheistic religion is how it reacted to the pagan religions with which it came into contact. The Book of Exodus sets forth the deliverance from Egypt in the context of a spiritual struggle with the pagan Egyptian gods. The ten plagues became not only a judgment upon the polytheistic Egyptian religion, but also a clear contest between Yahweh and the Egyptian gods in order that all might understand who is Lord.

Egyptian religion, like other ancient religions, had a degree of relationship to the life cycle of the earth. It also was closely tied into the Nile Valley. The very elements of Egyptian religion became vulnerable in the drama of Israel's exodus from Egypt. Not only was the sacred river struck with a plague, but also the frog, a sign of fruitfulness, became a menace to the people. The sacred ram, the sacred goat, and the sacred bull were smitten in another plague and the sacred beetle became more than a menace for those who trusted in its divinity. Ra, the sun god, was struck down by the plague of darkness and, finally, the god of life was denounced in the death plague.[2]

---

*"Yahweh" is the Hebrew proper name of Israel's covenant God.

In preparation for the death plague, the children of Israel were commanded to kill a faultless male lamb during its first year of life and place its blood upon the sideposts and upon the lintel beam that ran across the top of the doorway of their house. The blood was to be placed between 3:00 p.m. and 5:00 p.m. On the fourteenth day of the month of Nisan a special meal was to be prepared and eaten. This meal consisted of the roasted meat of the lamb, previously slaughtered; unleavened bread because they did not have time to wait for dough to leaven, indicating the symbolic haste with which the Israelites were to leave Egypt; and bitter herbs to remind them of the bitterness of the Egyptian bondage. This passover meal has been observed throughout most of Israel's history to constantly remind the people of the meaning of redemption from Egypt. The redemption from Egypt not only involved deliverance from physical bondage, it was also redemption from the influence of the pagan Egyptian religion and a subjective experience of having God lay hold of one's life in spiritual deliverance.

The Exodus became a liberation experience socially, politically, morally, and spiritually. John saw a symbolic tie between the passover lamb and Jesus Christ as man's sacrifice for sin when he declared,

> Behold, the Lamb of God, who takes away the sin of the world!
> John 1:29.

As God delivered Israel from Egypt, so Jesus Christ sets one free from sin.

Once out of Egypt the children of Israel moved beyond the subjective experience with God to discover who their object of worship was. At Mt. Sinai their attention was focused upon the God who had delivered them and His demands upon their lives. As they looked back at Egypt they remembered what they had been delivered from. As they focused attention upon God at Mt. Sinai, they discovered more intensely who Yahweh is and what they can become in covenant relationship with Him.

Covenant and Sinai

At Mt. Sinai the children of Israel experienced the formation of a covenant with Yahweh (Exodus 19—24). Before the covenant was formed, however, they experienced a great time of celebration for their deliverance from Egypt which involved singing.

And Miriam sang to them:

> Sing to the Lord, for he has triumphed gloriously; the horse and his rider he has thrown into the sea. Exodus 15:21.

This Sinaitic covenant is not to be interpreted as opposed to the Abrahamic covenant, but rather as a step forward in its fulfillment. It was based on the words of Yahweh in which He offered them certain promises if they would obey His words. To this offer the children of Israel replied, "All that the Lord has spoken we will do" (Exodus 24:3, 7). Moses then threw the blood over the people as a ritualistic act ratifying the covenant. Again and again the prophets called the people back to this experience and the meaning of their covenant relationship with God. Only within the context of this covenant relationship were they truly God's people, a covenant community.

How are we to understand the ingredients of this covenant community? How are we to describe the people encamped later around the tabernacle courtyard? First, this community standing in covenant relationship with God is to be understood as a community of grace. God redeemed them from Egypt. He was their Savior. It should not surprise us to notice whenever the prophets talked about the covenant and Mt. Sinai they also talked about redemption from Egypt. They were redeemed to become God's people in covenant relationship. They were recipients of God's gracious deliverance. Once delivered from sin they, like all humankind, can then enter into a meaningful relationship with God. For in the final analysis, deliverance from sin means to enter into a covenant relationship with God.

Second, the covenant community was regulated by the law. But the law, as given at Mt. Sinai, is not to be understood in purely legalistic terms.

One day a family visited the tabernacle reproduction and when I had completed the lecture the father called my attention to the license number of his automobile—613. He told me this number reminds him of the law since this is the number of commands in the Pentateuch. Perhaps he did not know that 248 of these are positive commands and 365 are negative. From our conversation I discovered he knew much less about God's grace. Law was a part of grace. Before God gave them the ten commandments, He said,

> I am the Lord your God, who brought you out of the land of Egypt, out of the house of bondage. Exodus 20:2.

When God redeems a people, and when they are His possession, then He has the moral right to tell them how to live. On the one hand Israel had to understand that He was their God and on the other hand they had to understand the law was given as a response to grace.[3] Anderson correctly says, "From the very first, therefore, divine grace and divine demand, gospel and law, were inseparably connected in Israel's experience."[4] What distinguished Israel's concept of law from other Near Eastern religions was that her laws were intimately related to redemption and covenant. The law codes of the other nations were tied into human government and were enforced by human administration. But in Israel, political life was intimately tied to Yahweh since He was their King. The laws were enforced, not by human administration, but by an appeal to the will of the people to respond to the will of God as revealed through the law given to Moses. Observance of the law was Israel's response to God's grace. Likewise in our day, observance to the commands of Christ in the New Testament is not based on law as opposed to grace, but is a genuine obedient response to God's revealed will in His Son. One responds daily to grace by literally living under the lordship of Christ each day. If He has redeemed us, then we ought to obey Him.

Third, the covenant community was a worshiping community. Here is where the tabernacle and the sacrifices enter the picture. The tabernacle was not a place where people gathered for worship such as Christians gather in a church building to worship on Sunday morning. Instead it became the place where Israel offered ritualistic sacrifices and these became the means by which Israel worshiped God. It should not surprise us that immediately following the establishment of the covenant in the Book of Exodus comes the command to build the tabernacle. Israel's worship tied intimately into its covenant relationship with God. It had meaning insofar as it was related to grace, law, and covenant. For example, the Psalms speak of Israel's history and thereby declare expressions of praise and worship. The sacrifices took on meaning insofar as they expressed the individual's experience with the God of the covenant. Left alone to themselves, these sacrifices were without spiritual meaning.

The tie between Israel as a covenant people and the tabernacle as an institution of Hebrew worship must, therefore, be kept together. The tabernacle was not an afterthought on the part of Israel nor on the part of God. Rather it was the worshipful expression of the covenant community.[5] Even though the tabernacle narratives and the description of the sacrifices in the Book of Leviticus may have been handed down by oral tradition for several years before they were put into writing, they reflect the worship life of Israel as a covenant community prior to the building of the temple.[6]

Redemption, covenant, law, and tabernacle with its worship of God provide the background for an understanding of the meaning of the tabernacle. When these are put together, we have the kingdom of God as a people in community under the rule of God in the Old Testament. But this must always be understood against its background of redemption and covenant. John Bright sums it up well in these words:

> The Exodus was the act of a God who chose for himself a people that they might choose him. The covenant concluded at Sinai could, then, be understood in Hebrew theology only as a response to grace: man's *hesed* for God's *hesed*. The Old Testament covenant was thus always properly viewed, like the New, as a covenant of grace. This ought to be kept in mind. The strictures of Paul and others (e.g., Gal. 4:24-25; Heb. 8) against a covenant of works, however justified they may have been, were far more apropos to the Judaism of their own day than to the Old Testament faith. For Israel had begun its history as a nation summoned by God's grace to be his people, to serve him alone, and to obey his covenant law. *The notion of a people of God called to live under the rule of God, begins just here, and with it the notion of the kingdom of God.*[7]

From time to time Israel departed from this intimate

covenant relationship. Sometimes the people served the pagan gods of the Canaanites. Then, of course, there were times when they returned to the covenant, such as during the revival of Josiah. These departures had serious effects upon their spiritual life. Perhaps the most serious departure from the Sinaitic covenant came when they rejected God as their King in favor of a human being as a king and with it the attempt to be like the other nations (1 Samuel 8). As their covenant relationship declined, God sent prophets who invited the people to return to the covenant experience they had known formerly. Essentially the prophets called them back to the covenant. But the sad story of Israel's history is that they rejected the words of the prophets. Sad to say, God's people today often reject the Word of His spokespersons and thereby bring upon themselves spiritual decline.

Command to Build

"And let them make me a sanctuary, that I may dwell in their midst" (Exodus 25:8). In these words, spoken to Moses by God, we perceive the purpose for the tabernacle, namely, that God might *dwell* in their midst. Moses, having been well educated, and having had access to one of the best libraries in the ancient world (Acts 7:22), was the one to whom was given divine instructions on how to build the tabernacle (Exodus 25-31, 35-40). In fact, he not only received specific plans for various parts of the tabernacle, but the entire structure was to be constructed according to a pattern shown to Moses while on Mt. Sinai (Exodus 25:9, 40; 26:30; Numbers 8:4; Acts 7:44; Hebrews 8:2, 5). Many interpreters have speculated endlessly regarding what Moses saw at Mt. Sinai; they are mere speculations, however. Let us simply affirm that the tabernacle was divinely designed and be content.

Materials for the building came from the acacia tree and from the spoils of the Egyptians which the children of Israel brought out of Egypt.

> The people of Israel had also done as Moses told them, for they had asked of the Egyptians jewelry of silver and of gold, and clothing; and the Lord had given the people favor in the sight of the Egyptians, so that they let them have what they asked. Thus they despoiled the Egyptians. Exodus 12:35, 36.

Moses called for a freewill offering from the people (Exodus 25:1-7; 35:4-9) to which the people responded by giving more than was needed. In fact, Moses had to restrain them from giving because they gave too much (Exodus 36:3-7)! Here is a lesson in stewardship for God's people today. A redeemed people share their resources gladly for the spiritual life of the covenant community. Of all the groups I have spoken to about the tabernacle, I have yet to find one that needed to be restrained because they gave too much in their given church's offering!

Bezalel and Oholiab were filled with the Spirit of God to provide leadership in design and craftsmanship (Exodus 35:30-35). Bezalel provided leadership in the metal and woodworking, while Oholiab provided leadership in making the fabrics for the structure. With God's Spirit upon them, the work was completed in a relatively short period of time. If we take the narrative as it reads in Exodus, we find the tabernacle was set up at the beginning of the second year after deliverance from Egypt (Exodus 40:17).

Some think the actual time of construction took only 7½ to eight months.[8]

A problem arises, however, when we look at the *tent of meeting* described in Exodus 33:7-11. This tent of meeting was built before the tabernacle. There are two views regarding these two structures. One view is that the tent of meeting was used by the children of Israel in the wilderness. It contained only a small tent and the ark of the covenant. Later, after entering the promised land the full tabernacle structure was built. A second view is that the tent of meeting was set up immediately after leaving Egypt and used until the tabernacle was completed at Mt. Sinai.[9]

People and Tribes

Already in Egypt the twelve tribes were formed from the twelve sons of Jacob or Israel (Genesis 49:1-28). When the tabernacle was built the tribes were placed in a special order with the tabernacle in the midst of the encampment. Numbers 11 gives an exact description of the encampment and the order. Rhind says,

> The tents were removed 2,000 cubits, or 3,500 feet from the tabernacle; just the distance that they were commanded to keep from the ark, when they crossed the Jordan.[10]

Various estimates are given by tabernacle writers on the total area of the encampment, but we cannot be sure of their figures.[11] We do know, however, the order of encampment.

On the east were the tribes of Zebulon (57,400 persons), Judah (74,600 persons), and Issachar (54,400 persons), along with Moses and Aaron. On the south were Simeon (59,300 persons), Reuben (46,500 persons), Gad (45;650 persons), and the Kohathites (8,600 persons). On the west were Manasseh (32,200 persons), Ephraim (40,500 persons), Benjamin (35,400 persons), and the Gershonites (7,500 persons). And on the north were Naphtalim (53,400 persons), Dan (62,700 persons), Asher (41,500 persons), and the Merarites (6,200 persons). (See Fig. 1.) Only the tribe of Levi, divided

Fig. 1. The Placement of the Tribes

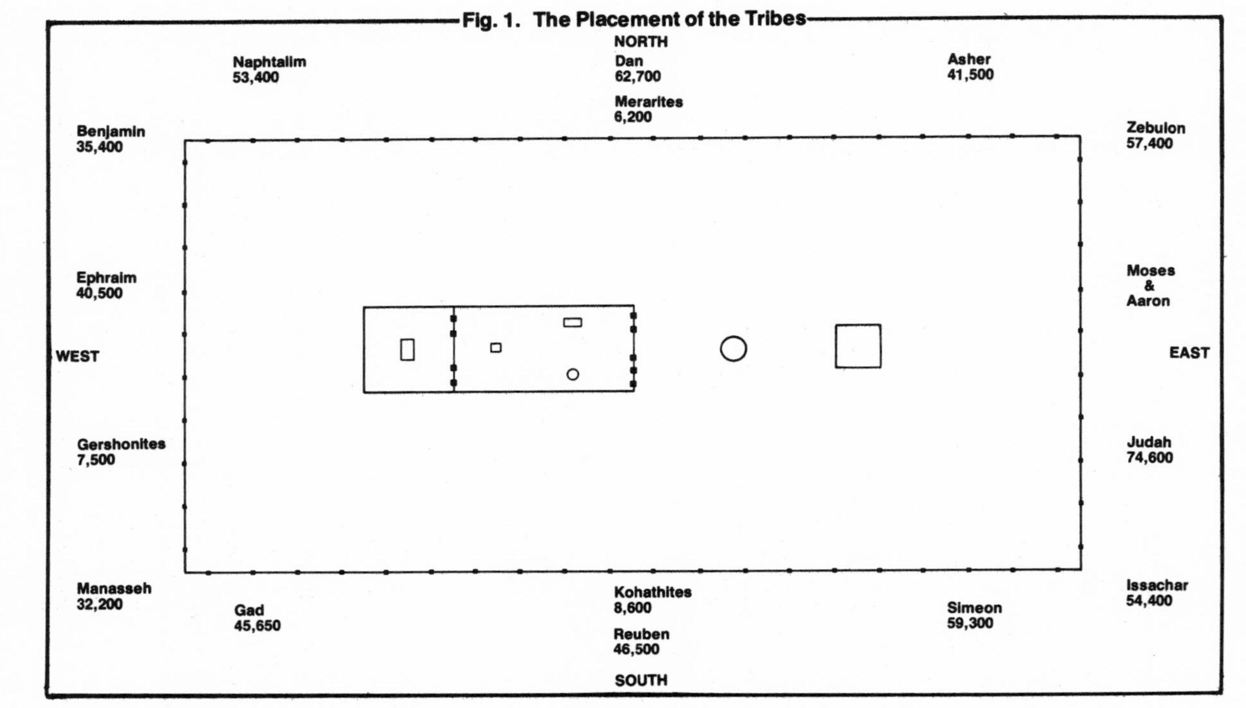

into the Kohathites, Gershonites, and Merarites, pitched their tents near the tabernacle for the purpose of keeping the non-Hebrew people from intruding upon the sacred area. These Levites were to preserve and to take charge of the tabernacle (Numbers 1:47-53).

And so it was in this type of encampment that the children of Israel looked back to their redemption from Egypt. Here they also looked at the present and focused attention on Yahweh, the God who had redeemed them, had established covenant with them, and had given them the law. Here they looked at the cloud and fire indicating His blessing, presence, and leading. Here they worshiped Him through sacrifices and offering and lived under His rule in a covenant community. God was with them and they were with God. In short, the setting is a people in God's presence.

The Courtyard

If we use the 18-inch scale for the cubit, we find the tabernacle courtyard was 75 feet wide and 150 feet long. However, the size of the cubit is debatable. James Strong argues that the cubit is 20.625 inches.[12] Upon further investigation one discovers in ancient times there existed a royal cubit measuring about 20.6 inches and an ordinary cubit used for commerce estimated between 16 and 18 inches. Normally the cubit covered the distance between one's elbow and the end of the middle finger. Perhaps the best evidence comes from the Siloam inscription and the tombs in Palestine which indicate an average length cubit of 17.6 inches.[13] For practical purposes, I have chosen the 18-inch scale for the cubit both in constructing the tabernacle and in the following description.

Obviously, the courtyard was open on the eastern half

Fig. 2. The Courtyard

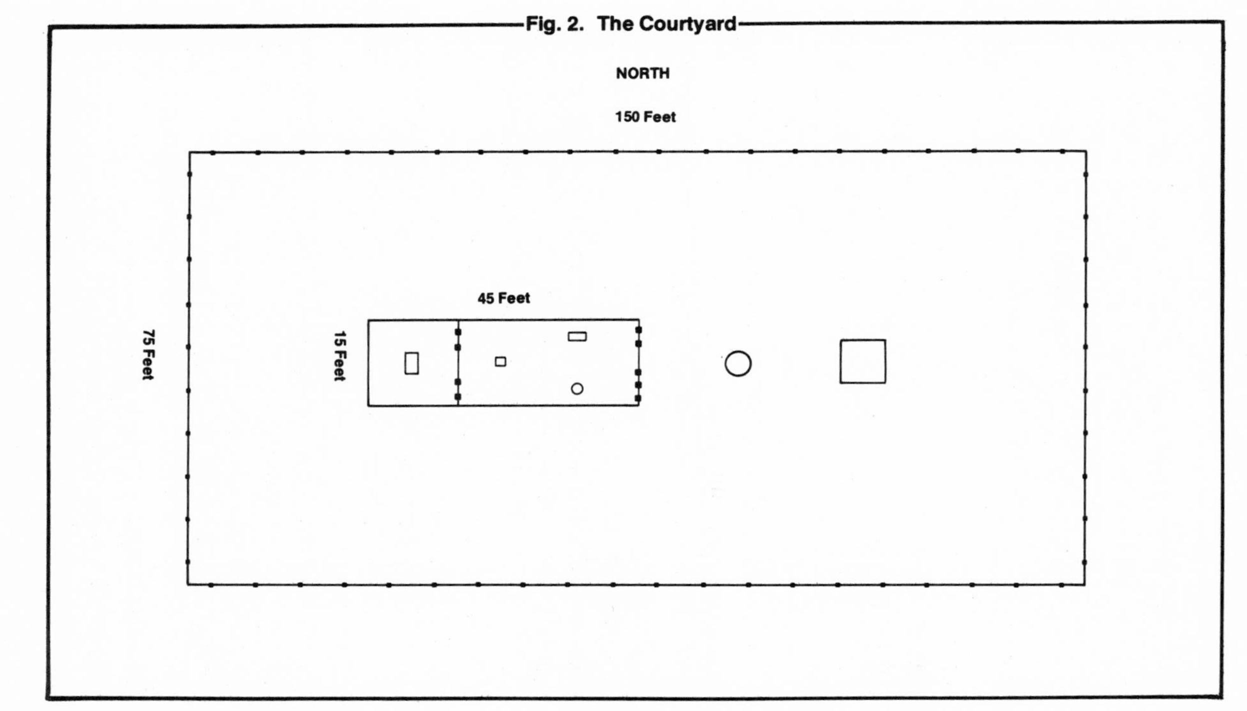

where the brazen altar and laver stood. The main tabernacle structure stood on the western half measuring 15 feet wide, 15 feet high, and 45 feet long. Since the main tabernacle building began at the center of the courtyard, an open space existed on the west side of the tabernacle measuring 30 feet from the edge of the structure to the courtyard fence. With this kind of arrangement, the brazen altar may have stood near the middle of the eastern half of the courtyard and the ark of the covenant near the middle of the western half of the courtyard (See Fig. 2 on page 31.)

Fence

At the outer edge of the courtyard stood a fence to keep persons away from God's holy presence. This fence consisted of 60 pillars, each 7½ feet high, arranged with twenty pillars on the north edge of the courtyard, twenty on the south edge, ten on the west edge, and ten on the east edge. Each pillar was spaced a distance of 7½ feet apart and consisted of acacia wood overlaid with brass (Exodus 38:10, 11). (See Fig. 3.) The pillars were placed in sockets of brass and had silver crowns sometimes called capitals.

Each pillar had a ring or hook on two opposite sides near its top into which a cord fastened that ran to a brass pin or stake in the ground to hold that pillar secure (Exodus 27:19; 38:20). In addition each pillar had a hook on one side which held the fillet, similar to a curtain rod, that ran from pillar to pillar and upon which the curtain itself was hung. Near the base of the pillars the curtain fastened to another hook.

The curtain itself was woven with enough air space between the weave for the wind to pass through. Levine says, "Had the hangings been woven solidly, they would have constitued a resistance to the wind, pulling and throwing the wall over."[14]

Fig. 3. The Pillars of the Court

To the average Israelite the fence marked his own limitations. Over its top stood the shining silver chapiters on each pillar; a metal reminding him of the cost of redemption, since it came as ransom money from the men above twenty years of age. But the white linen curtain marked his boundary as well. In fact, it was so high, 7½ feet, that no one in Israel was able to look over it. One can imagine the inner sense of anguish an average Israelite felt when he looked at the fence and discovered his own exclusion from God. To be so near to God and yet so far away could only leave one with a great sense of loneliness in his inner being.

Generally speaking the Israelites did not pass into the courtyard. Only the priests and Levites were allowed inside the fenced area. However, on specific occasions, such as preparing peace and wave offerings, and at certain times they could assemble in the areas between the brazen altar and the gate of the fence.[15] But these occasions were rare, indeed, leaving them with a sense of frustration. The purpose for the tabernacle was that God might dwell in their presence, but for all practical purposes they found themselves separated from Him. That same alienation describes modern man apart from Jesus Christ.

Gate

Entrance into the courtyard came by a gate located at the center of the eastern edge of the courtyard. It was twenty cubits, or 30 feet, in length. The gate consisted of four pillars with a screen of white fine twined linen hanging upon them. The linen was embroidered with fine needlework in blue, purple, and scarlet against a background of white (Exodus 27:16; 38:18). These four colors provided the color scheme for the entire tabernacle. Attempts have been made by some authors to view these colors as symbolic of the work of

Christ: blue with His heavenly character, white with His holiness, scarlet with His blood, and purple with His royalty. In fact, some go so far as to identify the four pillars of the gate with the four Gospel writers! Needless to say this kind of allegorizing places one's interpretation in the realm of imagination rather than that of fact.

A special type of workmanship was used, according to Haran, indicating something of the quality of the fabric.[16] This screen, like the screen at the door of the tabernacle and the veil itself, hung loosely so those entering and leaving the courtyard could simply lift it up and pass underneath.

No doubt the priests passed it often. The Levites also passed through the gate at regular times. But for the average Israelite to pass underneath the screen at the gate was an exciting experience of moving closer to God's presence. It marked a step in the direction of access to God. Little do Christians recognize the meaning of such an adventure because we experience God's presence daily. But for the children of Israel to go through the gate marked a holy moment, a time when the Israelite gave himself in the act of worship.

2
BRAZEN ALTAR AND LAVER

Inside the courtyard two articles of tabernacle furniture stood, the brazen altar where most of the animal sacrifices were offered, and the laver for cleansing. Both of these articles of furniture helped provide access to God. The Israelite, separated from God because of sin, experienced a limited degree of access to God through the priest as his representative. By offering animal sacrifices at the altar and by the cleansing of the priests at the laver, the Israelite believed something was taking place between himself and God.

Brazen Altar

Between the gate at the courtyard and the door of the tabernacle stood the brazen altar. The altar consisted of acacia wood, a species of the Shitta tree which apparently grew in the Sinai area. This acacia tree survived and grew in dry soil. Being a product of the desert, it stands in great contrast to the olive and cedar woods which workmen used in constructing the temple of Solomon.[1]

The brazen altar, its dimensions 4½ feet high and 7½ feet square, had metal overlaying its acacia wood. While many English translations identify its metal as brass or bronze, I am inclined to agree with such writers as Haran, Gooding,

Fig. 4. The Brazen Altar

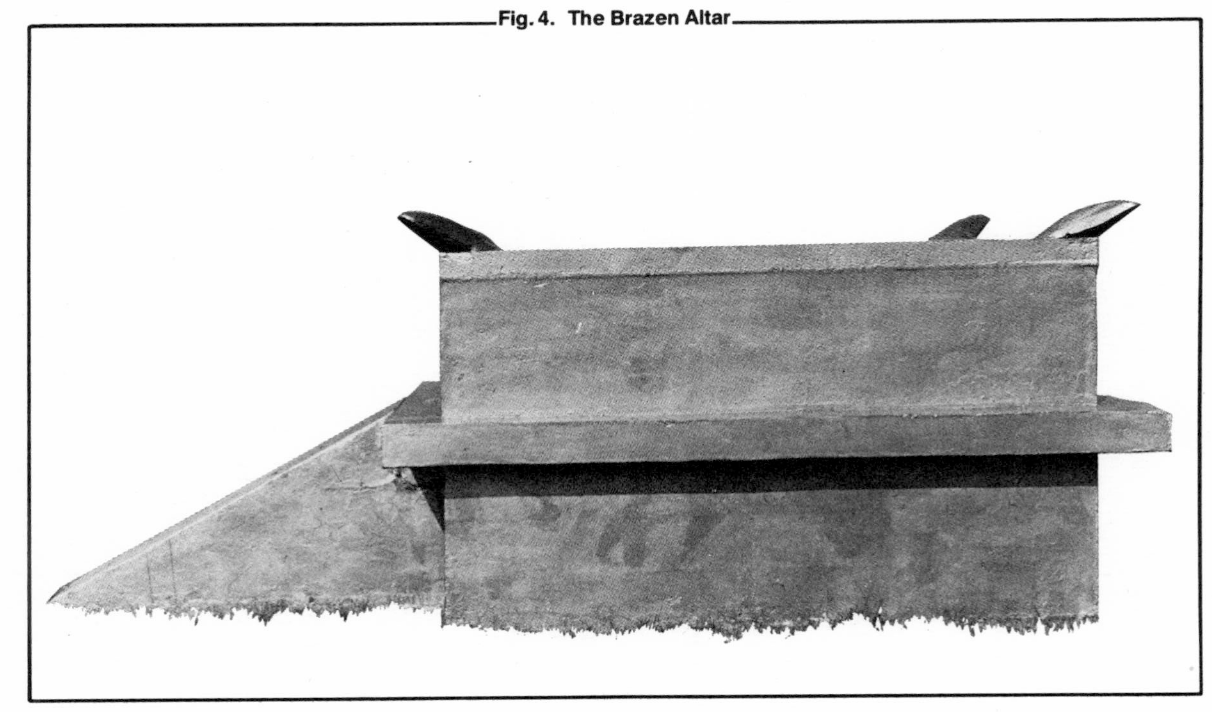

and Levine who identify it as copper. At the top of each of the four corners a horn pointed upward and outward (see Fig. 4 on page 37).

In some of the sacrifices blood was applied to these four horns, thereby carrying out the function of propitiation, that is, holding back God's wrath and granting a redemptive effect (Exodus 29:12). On other occasions the sacrifice was tied to the horns (Psalm 118:27). Later in Israel's experience the horn served as a symbol of grace for one who was fleeing for his life. If one was pursued for having committed a crime, he could lay hold of the horns of the altar and thereby escape punishment (1 Kings 2:28). The horns also symbolized power as one reads in 1 Samuel 2:1, 10; 2 Samuel 22:3; Psalm 89:17; 112:9.

A ramp protruded out from the south side of this altar for the priests to carry animal sacrifices to the top and place them upon its grate for burning. About mid-way up, on the inside of this altar, a grate was fastened upon which the sacrificial animal rested. Beneath this grate burned the holy fire which consumed the sacrifice making the bottom half of the inside of the altar a hearth. On its eastern side a small door opened so the priests could remove the ashes which fell as the sacrifice burned. On the outside, at its midpoint, a ledge was built around the four sides of the altar upon which the priests walked as they carried the sacrifice and placed it upon the grate for burning (see Fig. 4 on page 37).

At each of the four corners a ring was fastened through which a rod or stave was placed for carrying the altar as the children of Israel journeyed through the wilderness and into the promised land. The tools used by the priests for maneuvering the sacrifice and disposing of its ashes were pails, scrapers, basins, forks, and firepans (Exodus 27:3; 38:3; 40:10; Numbers 4:14).

Two holy places surrounded the altar. On its east side, between the altar and the gate, was the first holy spot known as "the entrance to the tent of meeting." Here the individual laid his hands on the sacrifice. Here is where the peace offering was slaughtered (Leviticus 3:2, 8, 13) and where the breasts were waved as a "wave offering before the Lord" (Leviticus 7:29-30; 14:11-12; 23-24; Numbers 5:16-25; 6:10-20; 8:9-13). Also, this is the area where the people could cook the peace offering (Numbers 6:18) and in certain cases even assemble (Leviticus 8:3-4, Numbers 10:3; 16:19). A second holy place was located on the north side between the altar and the fence. Here the burnt offerings and the sin and trespass offerings were slaughtered (Leviticus 1:11; 6:18; 7:20). Here the priests partook of the sin, trespass, and meal offerings (Leviticus 6:9, 19; 7:6; 10:12-13, 17-18; 24:9; Numbers 18:10). Here also any garment was washed upon which blood of a sin offering had been sprinkled (Leviticus 6:27). And here the priests placed the ashes from the altar before carrying them outside the camp.[2] Later these ashes were carried outside the court near the eastern gate.

> And the priest shall put on his linen garment, and put his linen breeches upon his body, and he shall take up the ashes to which the fire has consumed the burnt offering on the altar, and put them beside the altar. Then he shall put off his garments, and put on other garments, and carry forth the ashes outside the camp to a clean place. Leviticus 6:10, 11.

Soltau says,

> This was a solemn and important ceremony: a peculiar dress was needed for the occasion, and a change of garments occurs in the midst of the occasion. . . . The priest when taking away the ashes would have the evidence in his hands that the penalty

> incurred by sins had been met, and the means of full atonement provided; he was handling the very record of death, and such a record of it as proved that a complete satisfaction had been rendered to God.[3]

Sacrifices

The early chapters of Leviticus give detailed instructions regarding various kinds of sacrifices, different grades within a given sacrifice in order to meet the various economic levels of the people, and the technicalities regarding how each sacrifice was to be offered.

The idea of sacrifice suggests something is wrong in man's relation to God and therefore life must be given up in order to right the wrong. The brazen altar reflected not only man's sinfulness, but also God's attempt to work at the problem of sin and alienation even in the Old Testament.

Thus the altar, with its sacrifices, became the place where Israel worshiped God in its historical setting and, at the same moment, pointed forward typologically to a final and complete sacrifice for sin in Jesus' death at Calvary for the redemption of humankind (2 Corinthians 5:21; Hebrews 9, 10). What was symbolized in the offerings at the brazen altar found its fulfillment at the cross since through that finished work of Christ the repentant person can now find reconciliation with his Creator.

The origin of sacrifice in Israel becomes a complex issue. Obviously we read of sacrifice as early as Cain and Abel (Genesis 4:2-5), Noah (Genesis 8:20-22), and Abraham (Genesis 22:1-14). Therefore, sacrifices were happening among the people of God long before the tabernacle. The more difficult question, however, is the relationship between sacrifice in other Near Eastern religions and the sacrifices at the tabernacle.

While there are similarities with other Near Eastern reli-

Fig. 5. Chart of the Sacrifices

NAME OF SACRIFICE	MATERIALS USED	GOD'S PART	MAN'S PART	REFERENCE
1. Sin & Trespass Offering	Male & Female of herd & flock, turtle doves, young pigeons, 1/10 ephah of flour	Blood on the horns of the altar (sin offering), at the base of the altar, on the side of the altar (trespass offering), all the fat.	Highest grade offering was burned outside the camp. Lower grade offerings were eaten in the holy place by the priests.	Lev. 5; 6:1-7, 26-29; 7:1-7
2. Burnt offering	Bullocks, goats, sheep, rams, lambs, turtledoves, young pigeons	All burned	Skin	Lev. 1; 6:8-13
3. Peace offering	Male & female of herd and flock, bullocks, lambs, goats	All the fat	Heave shoulder Wave breast	Lev. 3; 7:11-13
4. Cereal or meal offering	Fine flour, green ears, frankincense, oil, salt	A handful, part of the oil, frankincense	All the remainder	Lev. 2; 6:14-23

gions, the *differences* are even more obvious. And where there is similarity of practice, the *meaning* of Israel's sacrifices differs greatly from that of pagan animal sacrifices.[4] For example, Israel never interpreted its sacrifices as feeding God as the pagans did. Nor did official Israelite teaching allow child sacrifice or sexual rites as practiced in Canaanite religion. Though there were times when Israel's spiritual life degenerated to some of these pagan rituals, the offical teaching in Israel prohibited it. Instead, Israel's God was the eternal "I AM" who needed no food, who called for righteousness, justice, and worship as a spiritual experience of His children.

God always deals with His people within the entities of time and space. His commands come in a specific geographical, cultural, and historic setting. It should not surprise us, therefore, to see a rather close tie between sacrifice in other Near Eastern religions and within Israel. What would surprise us would be if the sacrifices carried the same meaning and therefore Israel's religion was merely a religion borrowed from the pagans.

But this is not the case! While the *origin* of these sacrifices may be found in the larger Near Eastern background, the *meaning* of these sacrifices were always changed to meet the demands of monotheistic worship.[5] Israel's religion came by command of God, but we must understand those commands in their historical context. (For more information on this matter see Appendix I.)

Sacrifice in Israel was more than mere ritual. It had to be accompanied by the individual's penitent heart and broken spirit. The sacrifice for sin needed to be the genuine expression of the repentant heart to be effective. Psalm 51 is a good commentary on the meaning of sacrifice in Israel. As H. H. Rowley says, "The ritual was believed to be effective only when it was the organ of the spirit."[6]

However, the broken or repentant spirit in and of itself was not enough. That spirit needed to be accompanied by an external physical objective sacrifice. Then it became potent. Rowley says,

> It is important here to realize that while sacrifice was thought to have potency, it was potent only when accompanied by genuine penitence and submission. On the other hand, penitence and submission alone was not sufficient for the cases where sacrifices were prescribed. They were primary as the condition of blessing, and it was always recognized in the true stream of Israel's religion that obedience was better than sacrifice; but it was not supposed that man could save himself from his sin either by his penitence or by his sacrifice. It was a divine power that reached down to save him in the moment when he offered himself with his sacrifice. The animal in itself could do nothing for him. But when its sacrifice was the organ of his approach in humble surrender and obedience to God, it became the organ of God's approach in power to bless him.[7]

By the mid-eighth century Israel's sacrifices had degenerated to mere ritual. The penitent spirit was not there in the offerer. Instead the people lived in economic conflict with each other and cared very little about the covenant. Therefore, the great eighth-century prophets lashed out against the sacrifices. Amos thundered,

> I hate, I despise your feast,
> and I take no delight in your
> solemn assemblies.
> Even though you offer me your burnt
> offerings and cereal offerings,
> I will not accept them. Amos 5:21, 22.

The charge that Amos gave, as well as other prophets, did not arise because they stopped offering sacrifices. Rather, it was because their spirits were not repentant. They were determined to do their own thing and forget God's way. There was no desire to turn aside from their evil ways. While they maintained such a defiant attitude, they continued offering sacrifices. But God, through the prophets, said "No" to sacrifice made without a penitent heart.

Only when sacrifice itself is accompanied by a true heart of repentance did the offerings and sacrifices take on potency. Several hundred years after Amos the Rabbis wrote in the *Talmud,*

> Sin offering and guilt offering and death and the Day of Atonement all put together do not effect atonement without repentance.[8]

In the Book of Leviticus one observes two kinds of sacrifices. First, there were blood sacrifices which obviously were only animal sacrifices. To qualify for sacrifice the animal must be clean and domesticated. Thus sacrifical animals were restricted to birds, bullocks, goats, sheep, doves, and pigeons.

A second kind of sacrifice was the non-blood or vegetable offerings. These consisted primarily of ears of roasted corn, grits, and flour to which olive oil and incense were added. Leaven and honey were strictly forbidden. The children of Israel looked upon leaven as akin to corruption. Honey was forbidden because it easily changed into acid.

A. *Sin Offering*

If an individual broke his covenant relationship with God, he made an offering for sin *(chattath).* This sacrificial act removed the sin (Leviticus 4:1—5:13; 6:17-23). As a matter of fact, it went beyond dealing with sins of the past. It included the idea that one would keep himself from sin in the future.[9] The problem as we will note later, was that the person did not change. The sin offering did not bring a change in one's internal character (Hebrews 9:9).

The type of animal and the method of sacrifice used depended upon the rank of the person who had sinned. If the individual who had sinned was the high priest or another priest, a bull became the sin offering since the guilt of the priest's sin defiled the entire Israelite community. If the leader of a community or tribe sinned, a male goat was to be offered. If the people themselves as a group had sinned, then, like the priest's sacrifice, a bull became the sin offering. If a private individual sinned, a female goat or sheep was used for the sin offering. And if the poor sinned, two turtledoves or two pigeons met the requirement as a sacrifice for sin.

Highly important in the sin offering was the use of the blood of the animal. The Israelites equated blood with the life of the animal. Therefore, blood became a requirement in the sin offering; in this manner the animal's life through the blood, was given up in the place of the individual person thereby creating an expiatory effect. In the sin offering blood took on far greater significance than in any other sacrifice with the exception of the day of atonement. If the sacrifice represented the high priest or the entire people, then the blood of that animal was sprinkled seven times against the veil in the holy place; it was placed upon the horns of the incense altar, and the rest of the blood was poured out at the base of the brazen altar. In all other cases of the sin offering (tribal leader or private individual) the priest placed the blood upon the horns of the brazen altar and poured out the remainder at the base of the altar. By this use of the blood, sin itself was absolved.[10]

In the case of the individual, the flesh of the animal went to the priests for food. But if the sin offering was offered for the priest or for the total community, the flesh of the animal was carried outside the courtyard and placed upon a pile of ashes, where it was consumed in fire.

B. Trespass Offerings

Like the sin offering, the trespass offering also had a special use of the animal's blood. This offering, called *'asham* in Hebrew, dealt with offenses or wrongs committed against other persons in the Israelite community (Leviticus 5:14-26; 7:1-6). Since it was offered in behalf of private individuals, the blood never went into the holy place. In the trespass offering the blood was *thrown* by the fingers of the priest against the bottom half of the altar. Whereas in the sin offering, various animals were used depending on the rank of the person, in the trespass offering only a ram could be offered[11] (see Fig. 5 on page 41).

Not only was the blood used differently from the sin offering, but in the trespass offering something entirely new arises. Here restitution is made with the person sinned against. The wrong is remedied both by the sacrifice and by repaying the one against whom sin is committed. In some cases payment of a fine accompanied the sacrifice (Leviticus 5:14-16; Numbers 5:5-8). Roland de Vaux says,

> if the rights of God or of a man had been infringed in a way which could be estimated in terms of money, then the guilty person had to offer a ram for reparation, and to restore to the priests (as representatives of Yahweh) or to the person whom he had wronged the monetary equivalent of the damage, plus one fifth.[12]

From this offering we learn that brotherhood under the

old covenant was so important that when sin shattered relationships not only must the breach of sin be healed by sacrifice but the relationship with one's brother needed to be fully restored plus an additional penalty of one fifth the monetary value for marring the relationship with one's brother was to be paid.

C. Steps in the Sacrificial Rite

Let us now trace the steps in the sacrifical rite to discover the full impact of the Hebrew sacrifice.

First, in selecting the animal, only the best qualified. It must be a clean animal because, as an offering for sin, the animal itself took on spiritual reality. Any defect disqualified its use.

Second, when the individual brought his animal to the gate of the courtyard, his hands were pressed upon the head of the animal while confessing his sin (Leviticus 1:4; 3:2, 8, 12). This act symbolized the transference of sin from the individual to the animal. Henceforth, the animal in sacrifice became the sinner's substitute.

Third, the animal was taken approximately twenty feet north of the brazen altar where it was slain. It should be noted that the person who made the sacrifice killed his own animal. The priests and Levites slaughtered only the animals offered in public sacrifices. In the sacrificial rite the animal's death possessed very significant meaning. It is a distinct act in itself separate from the specialized use of the sacrificial blood. Sin always carries the effect of death. Either the sinner dies or another must die in his place. As Lehman says,

> The death of the animal was the most significant act in the ritual of sacrifice. It significantly sets forth the forfeiture of life as the price of expiation.[13]

Fourth, we discover the sacrificial use of the blood of that animal.

> For the life of the flesh is in the blood; and I have given it for you upon the altar to make atonement for your souls; for it is the blood that makes atonement, by reason of the life. Leviticus 17:11.

The blood and its use at the brazen altar indicated the life of the animal now is given up to God. If God required the life of an animal in turn for the sin of an individual, then the use of the blood satisfied God's requirement and made possible a degree of redemption in the Old Testament providing the spirit and heart of the individual expressed repentance. God is not satisfied merely with the death of an animal. Forgiveness requires the *life* and not merely the *body* of another.

In the fifth step in the sacrifical rite some parts of the animal were burned at the brazen altar. The sixth and final step came in eating parts of the animal in a sacrificial meal. These steps are best discovered in the burnt and peace offerings.

D. Burnt Offering

The burnt offering *('olah)*, according to Leviticus 1, consisted of a male animal, small or large, or a bird for a poor person. The outstanding characteristic of this offering is the burning of the entire animal upon the brazen altar. Laying on hands and killing the sacrifice in burnt offering are similar to the sin and trespass offerings. Here, however, the blood was merely poured around the base of the altar.

Having used the blood properly, the one in charge then skinned and cut up the animal. Having given the skin back to the offerer, he next washed the rest of the animal including its head, intestines, and hooves. Then he cut the animal into four quarters and placed them upon the brazen altar for burning. Thus, this sacrifice is called the whole burnt offering. Sometimes this burnt offering was accompanied by an offering of flour kneaded with oil and a libation of wine (Leviticus 23:18). This sacrifice was normally offered twice a day, once in the morning and once in the evening.

Originally, the purpose of the whole burnt offering became an expression of homage to God as in the case of Noah.[14] But later, as the individual identified himself with his animal, it took on a deeper meaning. As the smoke of the burning animal ascended heavenward, the offerer sensed his animal is his own no longer. It is God's possession. In a similar act of consecration, the offerer likewise gave his own life to God for service by identifying with his animal. Thus, consecration of life to God expressed the central meaning of the burnt offering in Israel's worship experience.

E. Peace Offering

In the peace offering uneatable and fat portions of the animal were burned, but the remainder of the animal became available for human consumption. Here the family gathered around the table and in eating the sacrifice experienced fellowship both among themselves and with God. In this peace offering Israel's sacrifices carried its participant to the highest level of worship through fellowship with God. Kraus says,

> The peace offering is eaten by a community which can consist of the family (1 Samuel 1:4, 21), the clan, the tribe, a group of pilgrims, or a larger circle of the tribal confederacy. The idea and expectation that the meal eaten together will create *communio* is basic to this sacrifice. He who eats with another person becomes united with him and proclaims that they are closely

> bound together. The most valuable parts of the animal that has been killed, the portions of fat, are solemnly offered to God, and only when the fat has been completely burned up can the meal begin (1 Samuel 11:15), for now God himself shares the food. The *communio,* therefore, is twofold, the communion among themselves of those who eat together, and the communion of these same people with the *deus praesens.*[15]

Theologically, these blood sacrifices carried important meanings. Progress marks one's relationship with God as he moves from one sacrifice to the next. In the sin offering expiation for sin resulted in the healing of the covenant bond between the individual and God. In the trespass offering expiation for sin also took place, but here the individual found healing from his sin against a fellow member of the covenant community. Only when expiation moved on to full reconciliation by way of restitution did this sacrifice find completion. Thereupon the offerer moved theologically to the realm of consecration to God through the burnt offering. And finally the offerer reached the level of fellowship with God in the peace offering. In short, these sacrifices moved the Old Testament person from expiation for sin to consecration of his life to God, and to open fellowship with God.

F. Non-Blood Sacrifices

The primary non-blood sacrifice was the cereal or meal offering. This offering came in three grades; unbaked flour (Leviticus 2:1), baked loaves or cakes (Leviticus 2:4-10), and green ears of corn either parched or roasted (Leviticus 2:14). The flour had oil, frankincense, and salt mixed in it, but leaven and honey were forbidden (Leviticus 2:11-13). This offering became the tangible expression of giving from the fruits of the ground. It said, in effect, that the Lord's portion of the crops must be given to Him. The individual presented this offering before the Lord and then took a handful of flour and oil and burned them on the brazen altar for a memorial. In a similar manner the Lord's portion of frankincense burned. All remaining food belonged to the priests for eating, leaving none for the offerer.

In addition to the cereal offering, the Book of Leviticus describes the wave offering in which the breast and bread are waved before the Lord.[16] It also describes the heave offering in which the right shoulder or thigh, plus one cake of peace offering, are lifted up and separated unto the service of Yahweh.[17]

To the wave and heave offerings can be added the drink offering. Here the individual poured out wine before the Lord either at the foot of the brazen altar or around it (Leviticus 23:13, 18).

All of these sacrifices, blood and non-blood, take one to the heart of Israel's worship life. Through these sacrifices Israel expressed its faith to God. And, as noted earlier, insofar as the individual repented and the offerings expressed the true attitude of a repentant heart, they possessed potency. To a limited degree these sacrifices achieved their intended purpose of making possible a living spiritual relationship between man and God.

However, full redemption and reconciliation did not become a reality through these sacrifices alone. They pointed forward, symbolically, to the fullness of redemption in Christ. In a typological sense the promise of full redemption offered itself to Israel, but only in Christ does that promise become fulfillment, not only for Israel, but all humankind.

What Thou, my Lord, has suffered
  Was all for sinners' gain:
Mine, mine was the transgression,
  But Thine the deadly pain.

Lo, here I fall, my Savior!
'Tis I deserve Thy place;
Look on me with Thy favor,
Vouch-safe to me Thy grace.
—Paul Gerhardt

The Laver

A second article of furniture in the courtyard was the laver. We read about this laver in Exodus 30:17-21 where God gave Moses special instructions on how to construct it.

Apparently it consisted of the same material, copper or bronze, as the brazen altar (Exodus 30:18; 38:8). According to Exodus 38:8 the material for its construction came from the contribution of mirrors which the women, who ministered at the door of the tent of meeting, gave Moses when he requested a freewill offering.

Two parts are mentioned; a bowl for water and a base or pedestal sometimes called a foot. To our dismay, we discover no dimensions regarding its size.

Further, we do not know if it had a second bowl at ground level for washing one's feet or not. Olford, for example, holds to the view that it had a wash basin on ground level, so one could easily dip his feet into the water for cleansing.[18]

However, the present writer is inclined to accept the view held by Strong that the laver's bowl stood only a small distance from the ground so that the person washing could easily raise his feet and place them into the bowl of water or, by stooping over slightly, reach down and wash his hands[19] (see Fig. 6). This view seems to agree with practices of washing seen yet today among some persons in Africa.

One good guess is that it measured about two cubits or thirty-six inches in diameter. Perhaps the basin rested upon the pedestal no more than approximately eighteen inches

Fig. 6. The Laver

above the level of the ground. Some believe faucets on the basin drained it at appropriate times, but this is not mentioned in the tabernacle narratives nor are there any instructions regarding how the Levites transported it as they traveled through the wilderness.[20]

Its purpose, however, is clear. The priests used the laver for washing hands and feet. Obviously, after walking in the desert sand or working with the blood sacrifices at the brazen altar, washing both hands and feet became a necessity. With its metallic finish, having come from the mirrors of the women, it served as a place where one could place his foot in the water and see the dirt under his foot by the mirror effect. Thus, the mirror aspect of the laver pointed out one's defilement and the water became the cleansing agent for that defilement.

Two kinds of outstanding cleansing experiences took place at the laver. First, at the time when the priests consecrated themselves to the office of priesthood the entire body was washed here at the laver (Exodus 29:4; Leviticus 8:6). And second, the priests washed both hands and feet before entering the tabernacle, before ministering at the brazen altar, and before offering a burnt offering (Exodus 30:20, 21). Washing resulted in cleansing. Unless the priests experienced cleansing themselves, they were both unfit to carry on the service of the Lord and were liable for death (Exodus 30:21). Oehler correctly says,

> This is meant to signify that he who has to carry on the service of reconciliation must sanctify his own walk and acts.[21]

Thus, sanctification reaches into the meaning of the experience at the laver. But in the Old Testament the inward cleansing of the soul and heart of man was only typified. The full reality of sanctification comes through redemption in Christ. Titus 3:5-7 brings us to the heart of the matter.

> He saved us, not because of deeds done by us in righteousness, but in virtue of his own mercy, by the washing of regeneration and renewal in the Holy Spirit, which he poured out upon us richly through Jesus Christ our Savior, so that we might be justified by his grace and become heirs in hope of eternal life.

The term "washing of regeneration" as used in this

passage literally translates the laver of regeneration. The Greek term used in this passage is the same as used by the Septuagint translators in Exodus 30:18. Thus, a tie exists between the laver as the place of external cleansing and the experience of regeneration as the point where internal sanctification takes place. At the laver the water becomes the cleansing agent. In regeneration the Spirit cleanses. Therefore, the Old Testament ritual required to enter into the office of priesthood, the external washing of the body, now finds far greater internal spiritual meaning in the conversion experience where an initial act of cleansing from sin and setting apart of all believers for service to the priesthood takes place.

But the promise and fulfillment theme does not stop here. Two additional New Testament passages enter our discussion:

> . . . as Christ loved the church and gave himself up for her, that he might sanctify her, having cleansed her by the washing of water with the word. Ephesians 5:25b-26.

> Sanctify them in the truth; thy word is truth. John 17:17.

In the Ephesian passage Paul declares that the Christian believer experiences a cleansing experience by the Word. This cleansing is similar to the washing of water! Jesus, in John 17:17, indicates that one experiences a continual experience of sanctification as he immerses himself in the truth; and he immediately declares that truth is the Word of God.

As the Old Testament priests came to the laver for daily external cleansing, the Christian believer comes to the Word of God on a daily basis for daily internal cleansing. The Word has a cleansing and sanctifying effect upon one's life!

In the Christian walk there comes a daily internal experience of cleansing as one goes to the written Word to discover his defilement and rids himself of this defilement on a daily basis by applying the Word to his life.

In the washing of regeneration comes an initial cleansing from sin corresponding to the bath required of the priest at the laver before entering the office of priesthood. In the daily experience of coming to the Word one experiences a continual growth into holiness, a progression into sanctification, corresponding to the daily washings at the Old Testament laver. Christians are saints in process!

Gracious Spirit! Love Divine!
  Let Thy light within me shine;
All my guilty fears remove;
  Fill me with Thy heav'nly love.

Speak Thy pard'ning grace to me;
  Set the burdened sinner free;
Lead me to the Lamb of God;
  Wash me in His precious blood.

—J. Stocker

3
CENTRAL STRUCTURE

According to the biblical account, the tabernacle building itself measured 45 feet in length and 15 feet in width. It stood in the western half of the courtyard with its door at the midpoint of the courtyard, leaving a distance of 30 feet from the rear of the tabernacle building to the western edge of the courtyard fence.

It had compartments or rooms called the holy place and the most holy place. The former measured 30 feet by 15 feet and the latter a perfect cube: 15 by 15 by 15. This style of structure expressed some similarity with other temples in the ancient Near East, even among some of the pagans. The great temple of Artemis at Ephesus, for example, had a velvet curtain separating its uncouth goddess from the rest of the temple area. Other similar patterns are found in the ancient Babylonian temples. What is strikingly different, of course, is the object and manner of worship. Israel worshiped Yahweh, not the gods of fertility. Therefore, the entire structure became holy unto the Lord (see Fig. 7).

Upon the desert sand or stones rested the tabernacle. The absence of any description of a floor in the tabernacle narratives implies it rested upon the desert sand or stones as they moved from Sinai to Gilgal, Shiloh, and eventually Jerusalem. At first glance it appears that the floor itself consisted of holy ground since the priests could not enter the tabernacle without first washing their feet at the laver. But since the sand and stones were not carried with them from encampment to encampment, one concludes their holiness limited itself only to the extent that the tabernacle stood at a certain spot.

Thus, the tabernacle was quite different from the pagan temple idea in which the gods resided at a sacred mountain or spot. Israel's God was an active God who led them forward. He could not be confined to a sacred spot in the sand nor to a sacred hill or mountain. During the monarchy we know that the temple stood at a sacred spot in Jerusalem. When it fell in 587 BC, what happened to Israel's God? The prophets needed to help the people discover anew that God is not confined to Jerusalem. In the Book of Acts we learn that persons came to Christ from many backgrounds, races, and cultures and together formed a new worldwide temple of the living God. Today, the sun never goes down on God's holy temple, His redeemed saints!

Let us beware lest we confine God to sacred spots including cathedrals, monasteries, or Jerusalem. The God of Abraham, Isaac, and Jacob, the God of our Lord Jesus Christ, can be experienced by any human being anywhere in the world if that person comes sincerely to Jesus Christ in faith and repentance.

Though the spot itself was not sacred nor was the sand or stones on which the tabernacle rested considered a Mecca for everyone to go to, it did, however, have a functional use that was holy. In Numbers 5:11-31 we read that the priests used the sand of the tabernacle floor to determine if an adulterous woman was guilty. How often this ritual took place we do not know.

Fig. 7. The Holy Place

Base

A silver base rested on the sand floor upon which the boards stood for the main structure of the tabernacle. The silver came from men who were eligible to be numbered, namely, men twenty years and above. These totaled 603,550 persons. Each contributed one half of a shekel of silver for the tabernacle.

> The Lord said to Moses, "When you take the census of the people of Israel, then each shall give a *ransom* for himself to the Lord when you number them, that there be no plague among them when you number them. Each who is numbered in the census shall give this: half a shekel according to the shekel of the sanctuary (the shekel is twenty gerahs), half a shekel as an offering to the Lord. Every one who is numbered in the census, from twenty years old and upward, shall give the Lord's offering. The rich shall not give more, and the poor shall not give less, than the half shekel, when you give the Lord's offering *to make atonement for yourselves.* And you shall take the atonement money from the people of Israel, and shall appoint it for the service of the tent of meeting; that it may bring the people of Israel to remembrance before the Lord, *so as to make atonement for yourselves.*" Exodus 30:11-16, emphasis added.

With a little math one discovers that if the total number of men was 603,550 (Numbers 1:46) and each gave a half shekel, we have a total of 301,775 shekels of silver. Since a talent of silver consisted of 3,000 shekels, the contributions made a total of 100 talents and 1,775 shekels. From these 100 talents of silver the base of the tabernacle was formed with two pieces of silver under each of the 48 boards, leaving 4 talents to be placed under each of the four pillars beside the veil (Exodus 26:32). The remaining 1,775 shekels of silver sufficed to make the silver hooks, the silver tops of the posts around the courtyard, and the silver trumpets.

Apparently, each talent of silver nearly touched the next one since two pieces of silver stood under each board. Practically speaking, a solid silver foundation existed upon which the tabernacle boards rested. At the bottom end of each of the 48 boards, two tenons protruded outward into the sockets in the silver base (Exodus 38:27, 28) (See Fig. 8).

Far more significant, however, than the mathematical breakdown and the construction detail is the theological sig-

Fig. 8. The Tenons and Sockets

nificance of the base. As noted in Exodus 30:11-16, the silver came as a ransom "to make atonement for yourselves." Here, the concept of the costliness of redemption embedded itself at the base of the tabernacle. In addition to the costly base, we have the bronze metal in the courtyard and gold covering the boards.

Some interpreters of the tabernacle emphasize that the copper or bronze metal symbolized judgment, indicating that in the courtyard one stands condemned. They further emphasize that silver symbolized redemption as the key of entrance into the new temple of God, the church. Finally, they emphasize that gold symbolizes deity or that which characterizes the new follower of Christ in the new temple of God, the church. These interpretations, however, are simply gained by inference and one needs to exercise a degree of caution lest he say more than what these Old Testament passages intended.[1]

The cost of redemption was great at Mt. Sinai if the tabernacle required this much silver as atonement money. The New Testament, however, identifies a greater costliness for our redemption.

> You know that you were ransomed from the futile ways inherited from your fathers, not with perishable things such as silver or gold, but with the precious blood of Christ, like that of a lamb without blemish or spot. 1 Peter 1:18, 19.

Further, the Christian's temple, the church, now rests upon a new foundation—Jesus Christ. Ironic though it may seem, He was betrayed for 30 shekels of silver, the price of a slave (Matthew 26:15, 16). Upon this new foundation, and only upon it, does the Christian church rest.

> For no other foundation can any one lay than that which is laid, which is Jesus Christ. 1 Corinthians 3:11.

> So then you are no longer strangers and sojourners, but you are fellow citizens with the saints and members of the household of God, built upon the foundation of the apostles and prophets, Christ Jesus himself being the cornerstone, in whom the whole structure is joined together and grows into a holy temple in the Lord; in whom you also are built into it for a dwelling place of God in the Spirit. Ephesians 2:19-22.

Boards

The main tabernacle structure consisted of 40 boards *(gerashim)* each 27 inches wide and 15 feet high. These boards stood on end making the tabernacle itself 15 feet high. Six full width boards stood on the west side plus two corner boards cut specially for the corners (Exodus 26:15-25; 36:20-30). Each board had two tenons at their bottom which fastened into sockets in the silver base. Gold overlaid all the boards. Like the pillars around the courtyard, these boards consisted of acacia wood. (See footnote 1, chapter 2.) Over them hang coverings for protecting the holy place and most holy place with its furniture. Each board had a ring fastened to it on its outside surface and through these rings bars were placed which in turn held the boards together for a solid wall (see Fig. 9 on page 64).

At the two western corners rings fastened both at the top of the boards and at the bottom in order to hold the corner boards securely together (Exodus 26:24; 36:29) (see Fig. 10).

No dimensions are given in the Bible about the thickness of the boards, so we cannot be sure of the exact measurement. Josephus suggested they were three inches thick. Another writer suggests nine inches, but quickly adds, "But this is largely conjecture and cannot be proven."[2] Most contemporary books on the subject take the view of A. R. S. Kennedy that they were thick frames (perhaps 18 inches thick) but not solid wood because it would be too heavy to

Fig. 9. The Boards

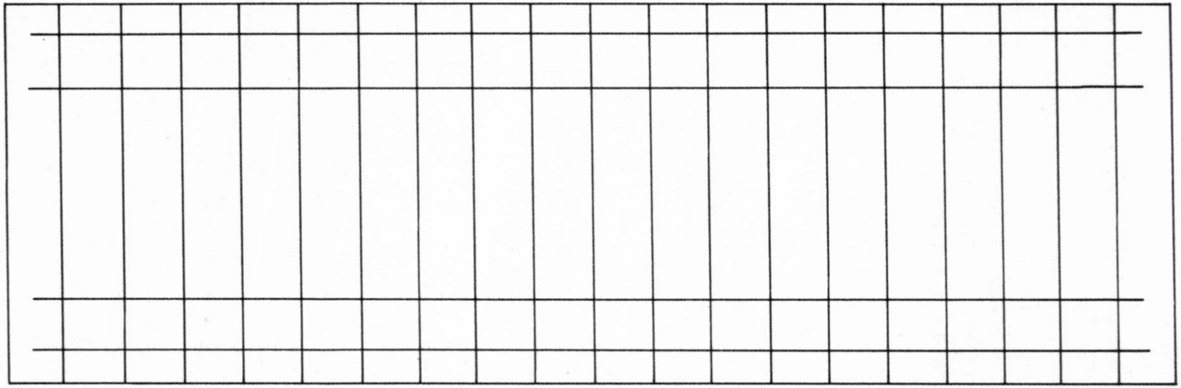

handle. Rather they had vertical arms joined together by crosspieces to produce a trellis type of construction.[3] Some Jewish Rabbis thought they were 18 inches thick at the bottom and narrow at the top, but that view is questionable.[4]

To complicate the problem further, we cannot be sure how the boards at the western corners fastened together. If the boards measured 18 inches thick and 27 inches wide, the corners came out with an inside measurement of exactly 15 feet, lending support to Kennedy's idea of the trellis type of board. James Strong suggests that the corner boards were cut into two pieces and were three inches thick, one piece measured twelve inches wide and the other fifteen inches wide. These two pieces were fastened together around the corner in a planned way that resulted in an inside measurement of 15 feet. I know of no other way eight boards could be used for the west end without measurements of either 18 inches or 9 inches thick in order to have a most holy place 15 feet wide at its inside measurement.

Bars

Five boards made of acacia wood overlaid with gold were fastened to the outside of the boards by rings (Exodus 26:29; 36:34). Two of these bars rested about 45 inches from the top of the boards and two about the same distance from the bottom (see Fig. 11). The fifth bar went through a hole in the center of the boards and could not be seen from the inside nor the outside (Exodus 26:28; 36:33) (see Fig. 12). These bars held the boards securely together and provided stability to the building. It is easily recognized that when they moved the tabernacle it took only a matter of a few minutes to pull the bars out, thereby unfastening the boards one by one and freeing them for carrying. The simplicity of the structure indicates the Levites dismantled it quickly but

Fig. 10. The Corner Boards

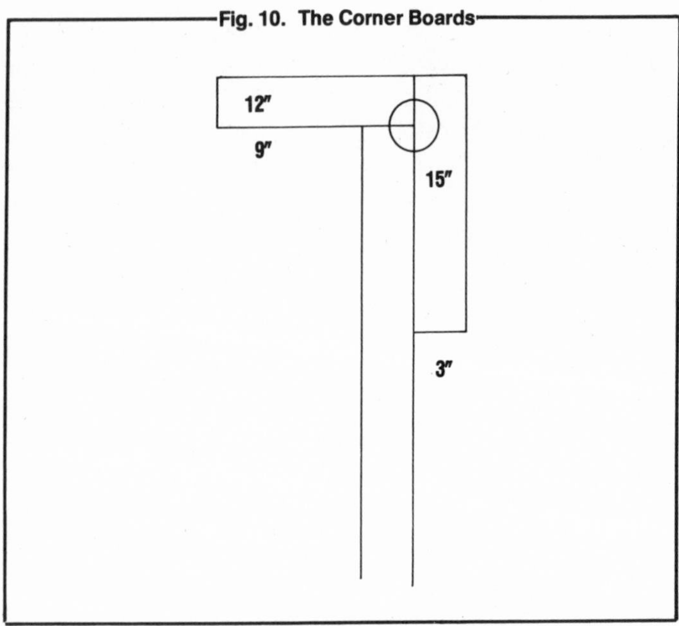

also quickly assembled it when they arrived at the new place of encampment.

Pillars

Five square pillars stood at the door of the tabernacle separating the holy place from the courtyard. Four pillars marked the dividing spot between the holy place and the most holy place. These pillars measured fifteen feet high, and consisted of acacia wood overlaid with gold. Architecturally speaking, the square pillars represented a pre-Greek type of column and tied in more closely to the type of pillars used in Canaanite and Egyptian construction.[5] These pillars were spaced apart unevenly so that the articles of furniture, particularly the ark of the covenant, could be car-

Fig. 11. The Bars

Fig. 12. The Middle Bar

ried out before dismanteling the entire tabernacle.

Three pillars stood at one side of the door and two at the other side. These pillars stood upon bases of copper or brass (Exodus 26:32, 36, 37; 36:36-38). Capitals decorated the tops of the five pillars at the door.

In contrast the four pillars dividing the holy place from the most holy were unevenly spaced with two on one side and two on the other with a wider space in the middle. These four pillars had no tops and rested upon bases of silver.

Near the top of the five pillars a fillet or rod of gold was fastened upon which there hung a screen, a fabric covering the entire doorway. Likewise, the veil *(paroketh)* hung upon the four pillars in a similar fashion.

These pillars and fabrics gave evidence of the separation that existed between God in His holiness and the people in their sinfulness. The gate, door, and veil each possessed a characteristic mark of distinction separating the people from God. The gate marked the separation between God and the tribes of Israel, the screen at the door marked a distinct separation between the priests, the Levites, God and the tribes, and the veil marked a separation between God and the priests and Levites. Only the high priest was allowed to pass beyond this important spot and enter into God's presence.

Coverings

Unlike modern buildings with rafters, shingles, or stone roofs, the tabernacle merely had four coverings over its top. These served as its roof and thereby protected the holy place in time of storm. Each of these coverings will now be described from the bottom one to the fourth or covering at the top.

A. *The Tabernacle* (mishkan) *Covering*

Directly over the heads of the priests lay the bottom covering extending across the top of the boards and down their external side to a distance of 18 inches from the ground. Instructions for weaving this covering are found in Exodus 26:1-7 and 36:8-13. Technically, it is called tabernacle *(mishkan)* because it rested closest to the dwelling of God in the most holy place (see Fig. 13). The term itself comes from a Hebrew root word meaning inhabitant. Therefore, the idea of dwelling, as the term implies, is a logical designation for this first covering since it covered over the most holy place where God dwelt as well as the holy place.[6]

Some tabernacle authors make a distinction between the first covering called tabernacle *(mishkan)* and the second covering called tent *(ohel)* thereby deriving the view that an A-shaped tentlike structure stood over and above the tabernacle. I have tended, however, to disregard this view in favor of my own interpretation that the difference in these Hebrew terms applies to the *kind* of fabrics used rather than their *shape*.

Unlike the veil *(paroketh)*, weaving the *mishkan* covering began with the white linen followed by blue, purple, and scarlet wool. In other words, the warp consisted of the very finest pure white linen and the weft of dyed wool in blue, purple, and scarlet. Cherubim were woven into it in the process. The veil *(paroketh)* also had cherubim woven into it, but the weave began with the blue color thereby showing a very distinct difference that clearly marked off the *mishkan* covering as less holy than the veil *(paroketh)*. Thus, the fabrics themselves identified levels of separation between God's holy character and the sinfulness of the people.[7]

This first covering consisted of ten sections forty-two feet

Fig. 13. The *Mishkan* Covering

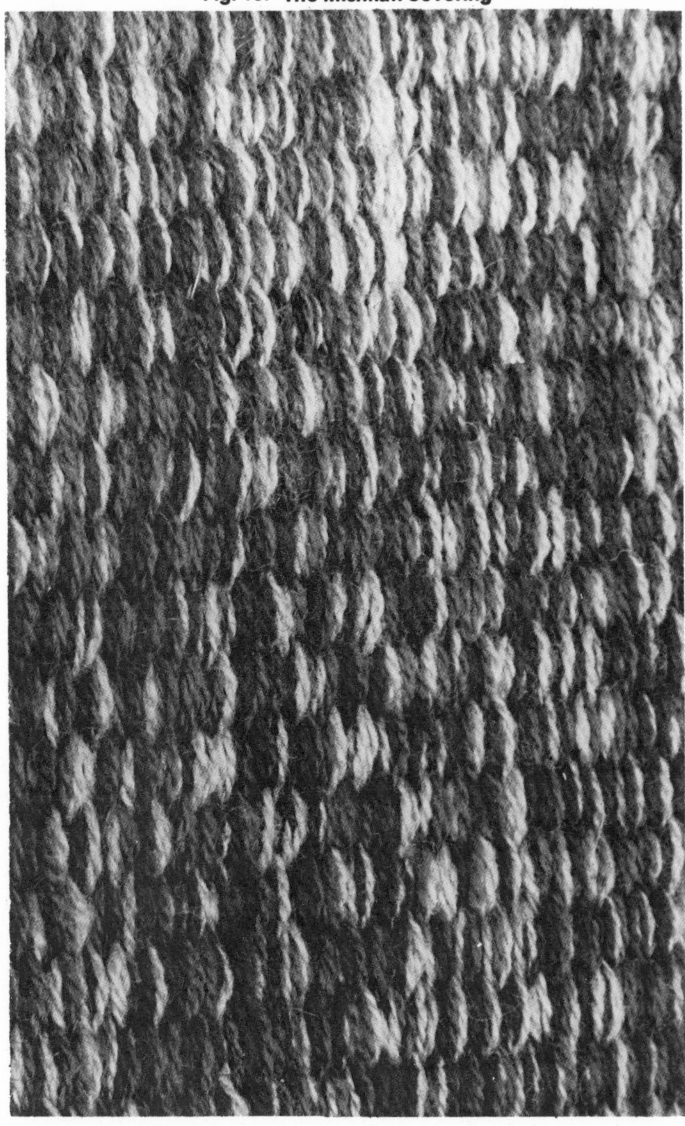

long and six feet wide. Five of these sections fastened together to form one large fabric forty-two feet long and thirty feet wide. A second group of five sections in a similar manner were sewn together forming a second large fabric with the same dimensions as the first. Then, these two large fabrics were fastened to each other by fifty blue loops sewn into the edge of each large curtain. Thereupon these two large fabrics were brought alongside of each other and fastened together with fifty golden clasps projecting through the fifty blue loops.

Fully fastened together, this first covering *(mishkan)* measured forty-two feet wide and sixty feet long. When placed upon the boards and pillars, it covered the entire top of the tabernacle structure and extended down the north and south wall of boards to a distance of 18 inches from the ground. On the western end it reached all the way to the ground. Its dividing line with blue loops and golden clasps came exactly at the point where the pillars and veil separated between the holy place and the most holy place.

B. The Tent (ohel) *Covering*

A second covering of goat's hair or goat's skin was laid upon the first covering. Technically, this second covering is called tent *(ohel)* having come from the black goat skin and hair from which tents were generally made in the Near East[8] (see Fig. 14). Likely the tents used by Abraham and the children of Israel represented this same kind of material.

Eleven pieces of goat's hair forty-five feet long and six feet wide were fastened into two large sections, one made up of six of the pieces and the other with the remaining five of the pieces. These two large sections were then fastened together by forming fifty goat's hair loops on each section and held together with fifty clasps of brass or copper. The completed

Fig. 14. The *Ohel* Covering

covering measured forty-five feet wide and sixty-six feet long.

When this second covering was laid upon the first covering, it reached across the entire top of the tabernacle and down the outside surface of the boards to the ground where it was fastened on the north, south, and west sides of the tabernacle with pegs and ropes (Exodus 26:18-25). At the eastern edge this second covering's first piece (six feet wide) doubled under (Exodus 26:9) so the wind could not blow it loose. Thus, the completed covering, when placed on the tabernacle with the front doubled under, measured sixty-three feet resulting in the last three feet on the western end hanging loosely on the ground. Thus the following biblical statement:

> The half curtain that remaineth, shall hang over the backside of the tabernacle. Exodus 26:12.

Whereas the division between the two main sections of the tabernacle *(mishkan)* covering laid directly over the pillars and veil *(paroketh)*, in the tent *(ohel)* covering the division between the two large sections laid three feet west of the pillar and veil. Since no mention is made in the account of a ridge pole nor any pillars standing higher than the others upon which to rest the ridge pole, it appears obvious that the top of the tabernacle was flat.[9]

C. Ram's Skins Dyed Red

A third covering of tanned ram's skins (Exodus 26:14; 36:19) was possibly laid upon the *mishkan* and *ohel* coverings (see Fig.15). No dimensions are given for this covering so we do not know if it simply laid upon the top of the tabernacle or if it also extended down the sides of the boards. Various descriptions regarding its size have been given by Rabbis. Maimonides suggests that it covered the boards while Rabbi Judah suggested it measured 15 feet wide and 45 feet long, thus covering only the top. But Rabbi Nehemiah felt the third and fourth coverings actually made up only one covering.[10] Perhaps it is best to refrain from conjecture and simply admit that we do not know the dimensions of this third covering.

D. The Top Covering

A fourth and top covering is *tahash*, a Hebrew term interpreted many different ways (Exodus 26:14; 36:19). Note, for example, these several translations: KJV—badgers' skins, RV—sealskins, RSV—goatskins, NEB—porpoise-hides, and NIV—hides of sea cows. In recent years many have thought

Fig. 15. The Top Coverings

Ram's Skin Dyed Red

Tanned Leather

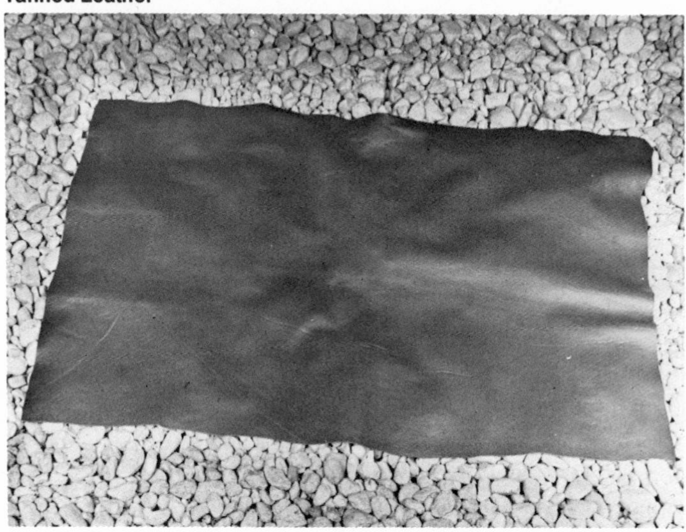

the Hebrew term means seal skin or porpoise skin which, perhaps, appeared blue in color. This view finds support in the Septuagint translation as well as the possibility of porpoises and seals living in the Nile and Red Sea areas. Dehaan, for example, writes,

> This outer covering of skins was made of leather, and the skins were taken from porpoises—not badgers as it is in our English translation. The porpoise was a marine animal, a sea animal which teemed abundantly in the Nile and the Red Sea. It is related to the whale and the dolphin. Its hide made excellent leather, Israel had no trouble obtaining porpoise leather from the abundant waters while they were in Egypt, but here in the desert, far from the sea, they could not obtain them. Evidently, the Israelites had stocked up on these leather skins when they left the land of Egypt, and for a very good reason, for they were to pass through a rough and howling desert, and the porpoise leather was the material from which their shoes were made, and unobtainable in the desert.[11]

However, Frank M. Cross takes a different view, namely, tanned leather. He says,

> By far the most reasonable suggestion is that of Bondi who connects *tahash* with Egyptian *tj-h-s*, Middle Kingdom *t-h-s*. As Albright pointed out to the writer, the phonetic equation is quite proper, and the word was borrowed during the second millennium to judge from the laws of phonetic change, thus fitting perfectly into the desert milieu. Egyptian *tj-h-s* is found as early as the Old Kingdom meaning "to stretch or treat leather." This would suggest then that the mysterious *tahash* skins were actually an imported (?) specially finished leather.[12]

While the evidence is not fully convincing, I am inclined to accept the view of Cross until more and better evidence is found. One reason for leaning in this direction is my practical experience of lecturing to many tourists, including members of the Jewish religion, who confirm Cross's view. The term *tahash* refers to an animal that is extinct today. We do not know its skin color.

These four coverings served as the roof of the tabernacle thereby protecting the holy place and the most holy place. Some scholars identify typological significance with each of these coverings, pillars, and boards, but I am inclined to refrain from specific types which the New Testament does not specifically identify. Only insofar as the coverings contributed to the central meaning of the tabernacle did they point forward to something greater.

Occasionally, as I lectured on the tabernacle, I discovered both Jewish folks and Fundamentalist Christians in the audience. Like eager beavers the Fundamentalists expected me to describe the red-dyed, rams skins covering as symbolizing the blood of Christ and the top covering, which they thought was badgers' skins, symbolic of Isaiah's view of the Messiah as one without form nor comeliness . . . no beauty that we should desire him (Isaiah 53:2). When, however, I described the fourth covering as leather, the Fundamentalist listeners felt dismayed, but the Jewish listeners nodded their heads in agreement. When the lecture reached its end both Jewish listeners and Fundamentalist listeners respected me. The Jewish listeners had discovered a definite tie between the Old Testament and Christ! The Fundamentalist listeners had discovered the Old Testament!

The church's one foundation
  Is Jesus Christ her Lord;
She is His new creation
  By water and the word:
From heav'n He came and sought her
  To be His holy bride;

With His own blood He bought her,
  And for her life He died.

Elect from every nation,
  Yet one o'er all the earth,
Her charter of salvation
  One Lord, one faith, one birth:
One holy name she blesses,
  Partakes one holy food;
And to one hope she presses,
  With every grace endued.

—Samuel J. Stone

4
HOLY PLACE

The children of Israel did not worship together in large buildings as Christians and Jews do today. Their worship came through the sacrifices. At times the sacred dance and sacred music occurred such as recorded in Exodus 15, but by and large, formalized music with a special choir and instruments did not occur until the time of worship at Solomon's temple.

Therefore, not much evidence is found in the Pentateuch of a group gathered for worship. This explains why the tabernacle was not considered a house of worship. Instead the children of Israel considered it a place where God met His people through the priesthood and sacrifices. God Himself dwelt in the midst of the encampment of Israel and through the high priest the people met God at the ark of the covenant on the day of atonement.

It should not surprise us, therefore, to discover that the tabernacle building is small. Despite its size, the holy place and the most holy place possessed magnificent importance. Here the sacred articles of furniture functioned in their appointed divine service. The screen and door, lampstand, table of shewbread, and incense altar each carried significance in the holy place.

Screen and Door

At the entrance to the holy place stood five pillars upon which a fabric hung measuring 15 feet wide and 15 feet high. Whereas the gate, marking the only entrance into the courtyard, measured thirty feet in width, the door of entrance into the holy place is higher and narrower. The gate, with its extra width, gave room for many Israelites to enter bringing their sacrifices to the Lord and to the brazen altar. But the door reduced the number who could enter to the priests and Levites, indicating only a diminishing number and holier group of persons were allowed inside the holy place. More directly the door implied that those less holy were excluded from coming closer to God while those more holy entered the holy place.

A fabric hung over the door called a screen *(masak)*, woven of fine twined linen with blue, purple, and scarlet (Exodus 26:36; 36:37). Like the veil *(paroketh)*, the weave began with the blue wool and not the linen, but unlike the veil it had no cherubim woven into it.[1] This is very significant because it implies a mark of separation. The further one moved away from God's presence, the cheaper became the workmanship on the fabrics. The screen marked an exclusion of many people from the holy place on one hand and the removal of God from a direct relationship with His people on the other hand. Christians believe that only in Jesus Christ were these alienating barriers torn down and through Him, by way of this reconciliation in Christ, man and God can come together in personal relationship. When giving lectures on the tabernacle I often heard people comment, "It made us feel close to God."

Whereas the screen at the gate of the courtyard fastened to the posts with fillets and hooks, so, too, at the door a fillet overlaid with gold ran across the tops of the five pillars and hooks held the screen to the pillars. As noted earlier, the pillars were square, rested on bronze or copper bases, reaching fifteen feet in height, and had special tops placed upon them.

Golden Lampstand

Six major articles of furniture stood in the tabernacle. Of these six, three manifest God to his people (lampstand, table of shewbread, ark of the covenant) and the other three deal with the people's approach to God (brazen altar, laver, incense altar). Perhaps it is best to say the ark of the covenant sets forth God's manifestation of Himself to His people and provided, to some degree, the people's approach to God. The latter idea found expression particularly on the day of atonement when the high priest sprinkled animal blood on its mercy seat.

In the instructions given for constructing the lampstand (Exodus 25:31-40; 37:17-24; Numbers 8:1-4), one discovers that the gold itself went through two processes of refining (Exodus 25:31). First, came the burning in order to make it pure. Second, a workman forged and pounded it into a beautiful symmetrical lampstand. As beaten work, the entire lampstand came out of one piece of gold. It may have been hollow indicating that its manufacture was no easy task,[2] but God gave a special filling of His Holy Spirit to Bezalel for craftsmanship in metal working (as well as to Oholiab for special work in textiles) in order to accomplish these tasks (Exodus 35:30-35).

The lampstand consisted of a central shaft and three arms of branches protruding outward and upward on two sides of the shaft. According to Exodus 24:33, 34 each of the six branches had three sets of almonds, knops or buds, and flowers and the central shaft had four sets making a total of twenty-two almonds, twenty-two knops or buds, and twenty-two flowers (see Fig. 16). The shaft with its branches rested upon a tripod which held it steadily, keeping it from falling over. It measured approximately 4½ to five feet in height and approximately three feet in width at its top.

Upon each of the seven stems an oval dish rested into which oil was poured for burning (Exodus 25:37; 37:23). James Strong says that:

> The lamps were of the type universally prevalent in the East; a flat, round or oval dish (usually of terracotta, but here of gold), with a handle (like that of a cup) at the blunt end, and the hole for the wick at the pointed end, while in a depression between is a larger central hole for pouring in the oil. In the present case we presume they were deepened into a cylindrical form at the base, so as to fit in the lamp holders at the tops of the candelabrum, and not easily fall off. The wick was made of thread of linen (from the cast-off pontificial garments, it is traditionally said), and the oil was from hand-crushed and cold-strained olives (Ex. XXVII, 20). . . . They are traditionally believed to have held each half a "log," i.e., a little more than half a pint.[3]

These lamps were ignited at the time of the evening sacrifice (Exodus 30:8). At the time of the morning sacrifice the priests filled and trimmed (Exodus 30:7) them. They were intended to give perpetual light (Exodus 27:20; Leviticus 24:2) which means they burned all night. According to Josephus *(Antiquities* III. 8:3), three of the lamps also burned during the daytime. Only the purest olive oil supplied the fuel (Exodus 27:20; Leviticus 24:1-4). By slightly bruising the olive, rather than crushing it in the olive press, the priests collected this special oil. When in the press, the oil did not reach purity unless the priest gently pounded the olive making the first drops of oil the purest quality.[4]

Care for this lampstand came by additional tools includ-

Fig. 16. The Lampstand

ing tongs, snuffers and snuff dishes, and vessels for oil (Exodus 25:38, 39; 37:23, 24; Numbers 4:9, 10). The oil was normally poured from the vessel or pitcher into each of the bowls on a daily basis. Snuffers trimmed back the wick and any charred part of it. These snuffers also put out the flame. Charred particles from the oil lamps dropped into the snuffer dish and were carried away.

The lampstand gave light so that the priests had clear vision as they carried out their duties inside the holy place. Seven lamps on the lampstand indicated fullness of light.[5]

But the lampstand means far more than fullness of light since light itself has moral implications. God Himself is light (1 John 1:5). In its Old Testament setting the lampstand not only gave light so the priests could see, but also represented Israel's God-given role in the ancient world of providing light to the other nations so that they, too, might perceive the one and only true God. The prophet Isaiah wrote,

> I am the Lord, I have called you in righteousness, I have taken you by the hand and kept you; I have given you as a covenant to the people, a light to the nations, to open the eyes that are blind, to bring out the prisoners from the dungeon, from the prison those who sit in darkness. Isaiah 42:6, 7.

How well did ancient Israel lead others in perceiving the one and only true God? Perhaps, at times others did learn about God, but the opposite also took place. We learn from the prophets that Israel itself became absorbed in the pagan gods. Nevertheless, Israel's role, in its divine calling, included becoming a light to the nations.

Only in Christ and the Christian church, however, does that role reach its fulfillment. In Revelation 11:4, the two witnesses, which may refer to Israel and the church, are "the two lampstands which stand before the Lord of the earth."

In Revelation 21:23, heaven is described as follows (emphasis added):

> And the city has no need of sun or moon to shine upon it, for the glory of God is its light, *and its lamp is the Lamb.*

Earlier John describes his vision of seven golden lampstands with Christ in the midst of them (Revelation 1:12, 13; 2:1). From these several verses in the Book of Revelation, one discovers that Christ is the light and the church is also the light. Christ's presence in the midst of His people, the church, makes the light shine in our contemporary world as He commanded:

> You are the light of the world. A city set on a hill cannot be hid. Nor do men light a lamp and put it under a bushel, but on a stand [lampstand] and it gives light to all in the house. Let your light so shine before men, that they may see your good works and give glory to your Father who is in heaven. Matthew 5:14-16.

How does the Christian church carry out its light function in the world? Perhaps, the prophet Zechariah's vision (Zechariah 4:1-6) provides a clue. In his vision Zechariah learned that the oil in the lampstand symbolizes the Spirit of God and the holders or lamps for that oil symbolize the recipients of the Holy Spirit. Accordingly, the Christian receives the Holy Spirit who produces the Christlike personality within him. As Christ receives honor, people are drawn to Him through the church. Nicholson says,

> The light referred to is not merely intellectual light but spiritual and moral illumination imparted by the Spirit of God.[6]

Light has a twofold function in the world. First, it points

out what lies hidden in the dark. People tend to shy away from this light lest their evil deeds be exposed. Jesus said:

> And this is the judgment, that the light has come into the world, and men loved darkness rather than light, because their deeds were evil. For every one who does evil hates the light, and does not come to the light, lest his deeds should be exposed. But he who does what is true comes to the light, that it may be clearly seen that his deeds have been wrought in God. John 3:19-21.

Second, light provides direction as the Psalm writer declared:

> "Thy word is a lamp to my feet and a light to my path." Psalm 119:105.

As the church appropriates the Holy Spirit, that Spirit in turn makes Christ the light glow within. Through the Spirit the Christian finds ability to walk in the path of truth regardless of the surrounding circumstances. At the same time this light exposes the wickedness of sinners.

Holy light doth fill this place,
  Spirit light our way to guide;
In the presence of Thy face
  Sin and darkness ne'er can hide.

Heaven's gleaming, fullness streaming,
  Life and truth for man is found;
Light pervading, never fading,
  Lighting all the world around.
—S. F. Coffman

Table of Shewbread

While the lampstand beamed its light from the south side,

Fig. 17. The Table of Shewbread

the table of shewbread stood approximately forty-five inches from the north wall of the holy place. This table, resembling a coffee table in many living rooms, measured thirty-six inches long, eighteen inches wide, and twenty-seven inches high. Like the other articles of furniture, it consisted of acacia wood overlaid with gold (Exodus 26:35; 37:10-16). The top of the table rested upon four legs which had rings and staves in them for carrying (Exodus 25:24, 28). A wooden border extended around the outside of the top edge of the table, approximately one hand breadth in width, which held the legs together in a framed structure. This border also kept the vessels upon the table from falling off while moving from one encampment to the next. The wooden border was decorated with a golden crown on both its top and bottom edges (Exodus 25:24, 25) (see Fig. 17).

Four golden utensils were laid upon the table for worship purposes (Exodus 31:8; 35:13; 37:16; 39:36). First are the "dishes" for the bread itself. Perhaps the shewbread remained in these dishes until the priests ate it at the end of the week.[7] Since one loaf was baked for each tribe, there may have been twelve dishes.

Second, are "pans" or "flagons." These vessels, shaped like ladles or cups with handles, held wine for the drink offering.

Third, are "bowls" which held oil. They had spouts for pouring the oil once a day into the lampstand.

And fourth, there are spoons each holding about a handful of incense used for sprinkling incense upon the new loaves of shewbread. In addition the spoons carried the incense to the incense altar for the special incense offering.

The shewbread itself consisted of a special mixture (Exodus 25:30; 39:36; 40:23; Leviticus 24:5-9). If the law of the cereal offering in Leviticus 2:1-16 applies to the shewbread, then the recipe called for oil mixed with fine wheat flour. Honey was strictly forbidden as an ingredient (Leviticus 2:4, 11). The dough, when baked, produced twelve loaves which Strong believes measured twelve inches in diameter and four inches thick! I do not think they became that large, but perhaps Levine states correctly that a frame upon the table held twelve shelves, each for one loaf of shewbread.[8] The bread was apparently baked by Mattithiah (at the temple?) on Friday evening (1 Chronicles 9:32), the beginning of the Sabbath, in order to appear fresh. It was placed upon the table on the morning of the Sabbath. The priests arranged the shewbread cakes in two rows with six loaves in each row. When the priests lifted the old shewbread from the table, they placed the new shewbread upon it until the next Sabbath (Leviticus 24:7). The Mishnah describes the ritual of changing the shewbread in the temple, which may provide a clue to the procedure at the tabernacle, in the following words:

> Four priests enter (the Holy Place), two carrying, each, one of the piles (of six shewbread), the other two the two dishes (of incense). Four priests had preceded them—two to take off the two (old) piles of shewbread, and two the two (old) dishes of incense. Those who brought in (the bread and incense) stood at the north side (of the table), facing southwards; they who took away at the south side, facing north; these lifted off, and those replaced; the hands of these being right over against the hands of those (so as to lift off and put on exactly at the same moment), as it is written: "Thou shalt set upon the table the bread of the Presence before Me alway."[9]

According to the Rabbis, the bread continued as fresh from the day the priests placed it upon the table until the day it was exchanged for new bread.[10] On one occasion David and his companions broke the traditional practice by eating the shewbread themselves (1 Samuel 21:4-6).

This shewbread stood before Yahweh always (Exodus 25:30). It represented a memorial and an everlasting covenant (Leviticus 24:7, 8). It clearly indicated that Israel owed honor to God for its life existence. The bread gave witness before God and the priesthood that God did and would supply Israel's physical needs. After leaving the lush Egyptian Nile area, with its bountiful harvests of vegetables, Israel now lived in the wilderness on quail and manna sent from heaven (Exodus 16:11-36; Joshua 5:10-12). This diet remained sufficient, but think of the complaining due to the same daily diet for forty years!

This shewbread, therefore, stood as a reminder that the people must fully depend upon God for their physical food; otherwise they would die. As an everlasting covenant it indicated that God can be trusted to carry out His promise of meeting their physical needs during the wilderness journey.

When Israel prepared to enter into the promised land with its grapes, figs, and lushful corn, Moses reminded the people of God's keeping power over them in the wilderness. He stated the shewbread's purpose in these words:

> That he might make you know that man does not live by bread alone, but that man lives by everything that proceeds out of the mouth of the Lord. Deuteronomy 8:3.

Unlike pagan gods, Israel's God needed no food. Instead He brought to His covenant people both their physical food and their spiritual food if only they obeyed Him. As the shewbread lay on the table each day, it set forth a constant memorial to God's faithfulness and the covenant of trust which Israel exercised in Him.

However, God also gave them a spiritual Word to satisfy their hungry spiritual hearts, just like the physical quail and manna satisfied their appetite. That came later in Jesus Christ who declared:

> I am the bread of life. Your fathers ate the manna in the wilderness, and they died. This is the bread which comes down from heaven, that a man may eat of it and not die. I am the living bread which came down from heaven; if any one eats of this bread, he will live for ever; and the bread which I shall give for the life of the world is my flesh. John 6:48-51.

As the manna in the wilderness met their physical need, so God's Word in Christ meets man's spiritual needs. One may partake of this spiritual food by repentance from sin and laying hold of Christ in faith. This comes not in the physical sense of eating, nor in the mystical sense of sacramentalism, but in a genuine spiritual experience of the new birth and a life of Christian discipleship.

Further, the shewbread pointed forward to that divine fellowship experienced between God and His people. The pagan gods did not speak or talk, but the true God of heaven is a living God who communicates with His people and dwells among them as they gather together for the communion service. As Christians eat around the communion table, they experience a sense of covenant community within their common bond of life in Christ. The Apostle Paul wrote:

> Because there is one bread, we who are many are one body, for we all partake of the one bread. 1 Corinthians 10:17.

A grand climax awaits the Christian church when as a bride the church sits with Christ its bridegroom at the marriage supper of the lamb (Revelations 19:9). Here the covenant of the shewbread in the tabernacle reaches its ultimate climax.

On Thy holy bread we feed,
  Hunger never more to know;
Thou suppliest all our need;
  Father, whither shall we go?

Ne'er forsaking, here partaking
  Bread our souls to satisfy;
Here abiding and confiding,
  We shall never want nor die.
—S. F. Coffman

The Incense Altar

At the west end of the holy place near the veil stood the incense altar. It measured thirty-six inches high and eighteen inches square (Exodus 30:1-10; 37:25-28). Four horns of acacia wood overlaid with gold protruded from the four top corners (Exodus 30:2, 3; 37:26). A rim of gold stood around the top edge of the altar (Exodus 30:3; 37:26) and two rings were fastened under this rim of gold on opposite corners for the staves to go through for transporting it from one encampment to the next (see Fig. 18). Apparently the rings fastened on opposite corners so that the staves, when through the rings, were diagonal. On the other articles of furniture there were two rings for each stave, but the incense altar had only one ring per stave.

No utensils are identified for use here at this altar, although Numbers 4:12 indicates utensils at this altar were wrapped in a blue cloth, then covered with a goat's skin, and placed in a carrying frame as the Levites moved the tabernacle.

In contrast to the brazen altar, where many different kinds of animal sacrifices served as offerings, here at the incense altar only incense was to be offered. The procedure involved taking coals of fire from the brazen altar and plac-

Fig. 18. The Incense Altar

ing them upon this altar after which incense was spread over these coals of fire and burned.

On one occasion Nadab and Abihu, two foolish sons of Aaron, offered incense with fire other than that from the brazen altar. Immediately the Lord struck them dead because of their disobedience (Leviticus 10:1, 2).

The ritual of offering incense is described as follows by Strong:

> The incense was burned twice a day (i.e., at the time of the morning and evening sacrifice) on the altar of incense by 3 priests (in the later age we learned from the Talmudic writers; but doubtless in a similar manner to the same act performed once a year by the High-priest alone upon the Mercyseat, Leviticus xvi: 11, 12), one of whom took away the golden fire pan

> and ashes of the preceding offering, another brought in a fresh pan of live coals from the great altar, while the third performed the fuming by throwing upon the coals successive pinches of the incense, of which he carried a double fistful in the hollow of his left hand.[11]

Of course, on the day of atonement Aaron placed blood of the sin offering upon the four horns of this incense altar for the purpose of making atonement (Exodus 30:10; Leviticus 16:16, 20).

Incense used at this altar consisted of four ingredients; stacte, onycha, galbanum, and frankincense. Stacte was a gum which oozed out of the myrrh tree on the mountains of Gilead.[12] Onycha refers to a shellfish found at the depths of the Red Sea which, when burned, gave forth an odor.[13] Galbanum was a resinous gum from a shrub which grew upon the highlands of the mountains of Syria. By making a small incision in this small tree in the evening, this gum could be collected since it oozed out through the night. It had a strong odor and ancients used it to prolong the smell of other perfumes. Frankincense refers to a sap which oozed out of a tree as soon as an incision was made. Ancients often used it symbolically in worship.[14] These three gums and one shell, when mixed together, formed the incense burned on the incense altar before the Lord.

This offering symbolized the prayers of God's people as a means of approaching God.[15] The psalmist expressed it well when he wrote:

> Let my prayer be counted as incense before thee, and the lifting up of my hands as an evening sacrifice! Psalm 141:2.

This incense altar stood nearest to the veil and thereby close to God. When incense burned its odor moved into God's presence morning and evening. Thus, the incense offering tied to prayer became a beautiful sweet-smelling odor to God. In Numbers 16:41-46 incense burned as an emblem of the intercession of the high priest.

In the New Testament this same concept arises. In Luke 1:10, Zechariah the priest burned incense in the temple while the people gathered outside for a time of prayer. Two passages in the Book of Revelation identify prayers of God's people with the incense offering:

> And when he had taken the scroll, the four living creatures and the twenty-four elders fell down before the Lamb, each holding a harp, and with golden bowls full of incense, which are the prayers of the saints Revelation 5:8.

> And another angel came and stood at the altar with a golden censer; and he was given much incense to mingle with the prayers of all the saints upon the golden altar before the throne Revelations 8:3.

It is this sense of the offering of sweet fragrance to God which was captured in the words of this hymn:

In Thy holy place we bow,
  Perfumes sweet to heaven rise,
While our golden censers glow
  With the fire of sacrifice.
Saints low bending, prayers ascending,
  Holy lips and hands implore;
Faith believing and receiving
  Grace from Him whom we adore.

—S. F. Coffman

5
MOST HOLY PLACE

The most holy place, where God dwelt, constituted the most sacred part of the tabernacle. It was clearly set apart from the holy place by four pillars constructed of acacia wood overlaid with gold and resting upon silver bases. The veil which hung on these four pillars further separated the most holy place from the holy place. These pillars were without tops and spaced unevenly so that the ark of the covenant could easily be carried between them prior to moving the pillars and boards of the tabernacle. A fillet, similar to a rod of iron, ran between the pillars near their tops upon which the veil hung by golden clasps (Exodus 26:32; 36:36).

Veil

A veil *(paroketh)* 15 feet long and 15 feet high, when hung on the pillars, fully separated the holy place from the most holy place (see Fig. 19). The writer of Hebrews 9:2 calls it a second veil to distinguish it from the screen at the door. It consisted of fine-twined linen with blue, purple, and scarlet wool woven by a specialized weaving method *(hoshev)* that resulted in the cherubim actually woven into both sides of the veil (Exodus 26:31; 36:35). This fabric distinguished itself from the first covering over the top of the tabernacle by a different order of weaving which began with the blue thread. This color combination produced a beautiful fabric. Levine describes the colors in these words:

> "Blue" signifies wool dyed in the blood of a conchiferous sea-animal called *hilazon*. The color is sky blue. "Purple" signifies a wool dyed red, in which are mixed white, green and black, as into a rainbow of colours. "Scarlet" signifies wool dyed red into which some white is mixed. "Fine twined linen" is white flax.[1]

When dismanteling the tabernacle, the priests laid the veil over the ark of the covenant, particularly the mercy seat (Numbers 4:5). In times of certain sacrifices the priest sprinkled blood in front of the veil (Leviticus 4:6, 17).

In Solomon's temple and in Herod's temple the veil was larger than in the tabernacle. Edersheim says,

> According to Jewish tradition, there were, indeed, two veils before the entrance to the most Holy Place. The Talmud explains this on the ground that it was not known whether in the former temple the Veil had hung inside or outside the entrance, and whether the partition-wall had stood in the Holy or Most Holy Place. Hence (according to Maimonides) there was not any wall between the Holy and Most Holy Place, but the space of one cubit, assigned to it in the former Temple, was left unoccupied and one Veil hung on the side of the Holy, the other on that of the Most Holy Place. According to an account dating from the Temple-times, there were altogether thirteen veils used in various parts of the Temple—two new ones being made every year. The Veils before the Most Holy Place were 40 cubits (60 feet) long, and 20 cubits (30 feet) wide, of the thickness of the palm of the hand, and wrought in 72 squares, which were joined together; and these veils were so heavy that, in the exaggerated language of the time, it needed 300 priests to manipulate each.[2]

This veil distinctly marked the point of separation between God and the people. While the screen at the door separated the priests and Levites from the remaining children of Israel, the veil separated the high priest from the other priests and Levites. Only the high priest entered God's presence in the most holy place, but even Aaron was limited to one day of entering God's presence behind that veil for the entire year, the Day of Atonement (Leviticus 16). Thus, the veil clearly set forth the alienation between God and the children of Israel, including the priests and Levites. In short the veil evidenced entrance into God's presence, was restricted to one person, and he in turn entered only on one day. Only in Christ did that alienation come to an end and reconciliation take place. In Christ the privilege of one is opened to all, the blessing of one day is available every day.

When Christ died the veil was rent physically and symbolically. Both Matthew and Mark clearly state that at the point of Jesus' death the veil was rent into two pieces (Matthew 27:51; Mark 15:38). Even more importantly the rent veil represented the broken body of Christ through which reconciliation with God is made possible. How beautifully is this described for us in these verses!

> Therefore, brethren, since we have confidence to enter the sanctuary by the blood of Jesus, by the new and living way which he opened for us through the curtain, that is through his flesh . . . let us draw near with a true heart in full assurance of faith. Hebrews 10:19, 20, 22.

While thinking about this access to God through Christ, Gerhardt penned the following words which Bach later set to music:

What language shall I borrow
  To thank Thee, dearest Friend,

Fig. 19. The Veil and Pillars

For this Thy dying sorrow,
  Thy pity without end?

O make me Thine forever;
  And should I fainting be,
Lord, let me never, never,
  Outlive my love to Thee.
      —Paul Gerhardt

Ark of the Covenant

In the most holy place stood the ark of the covenant.[3] This boxlike structure consisted of acacia wood overlaid with gold both inside and outside[4] (see Fig. 20). It measured forty-five inches long, twenty-seven inches wide, and twenty-seven

Fig. 20. The Ark of the Covenant

inches high (Exodus 25:10-22; 37:1-9). On each of its four corners a ring was fastened through which the staves were placed in order to carry it. These staves remained in the rings of the ark of the covenant at all times (Exodus 25:15). Like the table of shewbread and the incense altar, the ark of the covenant had a golden border or crown around its top edge.

Inside this ark were two tablets of stone containing the ten commandments (Exodus 25:16; Deuteronomy 10:2; Hebrews 9:4), a pot of manna (Exodus 16:33, 34), and Aaron's rod (Numbers 17:10, 11).[5] On top of the ark lay a solid piece of pure (refined) gold called the mercy seat *(kapporeth)*. It covered the law inside the ark of the covenant. Some suggest the mercy seat may have been of pure gold three inches thick!

From this same piece of gold two cherub were formed with wings covering over the mercy seat and faces directed toward each other (Exodus 25:19, 20; 37:7-9). We are not told the size of the cherubim indicating, perhaps, that the metal worker used his own creativity in forming them. Theologically, the ark of the covenant tells us about God's nature, His presence, His forgiveness, and His reign.

A. *God's Nature*

When the Levites moved the tabernacle, God's glory left the most holy place and went ahead of the people. The tabernacle itself, as a portable building, signified Israel's God was a living, active God who led them. He was not like the pagan gods of Egypt, Babylon, and Canaanite religion whom the people tied to a sacred mountain or another sacred spot. Yahweh was a God of action as the ark indicates. Fretheim says,

> In all of this it is clear that the cherubim-ark points to the mobility of Yahweh, the throne complex served to guard against an interpretation that Yahweh was confined to the temple or to Israel.[6]

Upon completing the temple and seeing God's glory filling it (1 Kings 8:10, 11), Solomon declared:

> But will God indeed dwell on the earth? Behold, heaven and the highest heaven cannot contain thee; how much less this house which I have built! 1 Kings 8:27.

However, tracing Israel's history through the monarchy and the divided kingdoms, one discovers that the people lost sight of God's mobility. They tended to confine Him to the temple at Jerusalem. When the Southern Kingdom fell and the temple disintegrated in smoke and flames in 587 BC. the people in Babylon inquired, where is God? While the Babylonian temples with their pagan gods flourished, Israel thought Yahweh lay in the ruins of the temple at Jerusalem. The prophet Ezekiel helped the people discover anew that God cannot be confined to the temple nor to Jerusalem.

When the church began in Jerusalem in Acts 2, this question still lingered in the minds of the people. Not until the gospel broke through in Samaria, among the Gentiles and elsewhere, did a small minority of Jewish Christians recognize that God is a living active God, present *wherever* people call upon Him. He cannot be confined to the temple, nor to Jerusalem, nor merely to the Jewish community. He is the God of the entire universe! Today He is known around the world in the Christian church.

B. God's Presence

God dwelt between the cherubim and the mercy seat. In fact, Israel thought of Him as a King enthroned at the ark of the covenant (1 Samuel 4:4; Psalms 99:1). Here God met His people through the high priest (Exodus 25:22) and because of the awe of God's presence, the ark of the covenant is frequently referred to in the Psalms as the place of worship.[7] His presence was so real that Israel believed that to be before the ark actually meant being in God's presence.[8]

Closely tied to the concept of divine presence was the covenant bond between God and the people. There God met His people through the high priest on the Day of Atonement (Leviticus 16). When they journeyed it went before them (Numbers 10:33-36), and it played a major role when they crossed the Jordan River (Joshua 6). It is mentioned about thirty times in the Book of Joshua. Newman says,

> Thus the ark continually bore witness to the covenant event and its meaning for the life of the people.[9]

However, when the people lived in disobedience to God and broke the covenant, God's presence departed from them. When the Philistines captured the ark it symbolized a broken covenant. Only by obedience to the law of God could Israel expect God's continuing presence among themselves. Therefore, as Fretheim says,

> The presence of God and covenant are thus seen to be closely bound up together in the significance of the ark.[10]

That divine presence also expresses itself in the fact that the ark was the place where God spoke to Moses (Exodus 25:22; Numbers 7:89) and Hezekiah (2 Kings 19:15) among other Old Testament characters.

A tie between the tabernacle and the Christian church finds vivid expression at this point. Two strands of thought, the dwelling of God and the people of God, come together in the church. The church is the new temple of God (1 Corinthians 3:16; 6:19; Ephesians 2:19-22). Through redemption in Christ, He comes into our lives and we experience the divine presence. As Moorehead says,

> He once dwelt *among* His people; now He dwells *in* them.[11]

C. God's Forgiveness

Of highest importance was the mercy seat at the ark of the covenant. While the law inside the ark constantly reminded the people of God's demand for holy living, the mercy seat affirmed their need for forgiveness. The word mercy seat *(kapporeth)* means "to cover" (Genesis 4:14; Psalm 32:1). The Septuagint translators identified it as a place of atonement, where God's grace covered over the law.

Law brought favor to God's people if they obeyed it. But if they disobeyed, the law stood as evidence that God's justice would be meted out upon the people. Only as blood sprinkled the mercy seat could these evil deeds be covered over and blotted out. The mercy seat, therefore, became an instrument of atonement. It marked the place where, by the potency of a blood animal sacrifice, God actually communed and met His people by way of reconciliation as the sin was covered over. As the high priest sprinkled blood upon the mercy seat, God's Word to Moses came to fulfillment:

> "There I will meet with you . . ." (Exodus 25:22).

Moorehead correctly says,

> For this reason the mercy seat is called the propitiatory (ἱλαστήριον) in Hebrew 9:5; because it was the place where the atonement was completed, where satisfaction to the divine claims were made, and where pacification was secured by the covering (atonement) of the sins of the people. Beneath it were the two tables, the ten Words, which testified: first, that God's government is founded on justice and righteousness; second, that Israel was in covenant relation with him; third, that their sins were ever present before Him, and that He was perfectly acquainted with their rebellious ways (Deuteronomy 31:26, 27). The blood on the mercy seat met the demands of the law and satisfied the claims of justice, for it covered the sins from the Divine presence, obliterating them altogether.[12]

It is actually more correct to say at the mercy seat *expiation* took place and at the brazen altar propitiation found expression. At the brazen altar the idea of satisfying a God who is angry at sin (to propitiate God) finds expression when the blood was placed on the horns of this altar. At the mercy seat the blood covered over sin thereby effecting reconciliation (to expiate). Perhaps the latter idea finds greater emphasis in the Bible, for God is not so much an angry God to be satisfied as He is a God of love moving toward sinful man to bring about reconciliation.

Thus grace and mercy represent the heart of God's dealings with His people. Perhaps, this is seen best in the ritual on the Day of Atonement described in Leviticus 16. It was the highest of holy days; so sacred that the people ate no food and did no work throughout the day. It was a "sabbath of solemn rest" (Leviticus 16:29-31).

The day's activities follow in this order. First, Aaron, the high priest, washed his entire body with water at the laver and dressed in special linen garments made only for that day (Leviticus 16:4). Second, five animals were selected for the day (a young bullock, two goats, and two rams) in addition to the regular morning sacrifice. Lots were cast between the two goats for the purpose of choosing which animal became the sin offering for the people and which animal the scapegoat (Leviticus 16:7, 8). Then Aaron killed the bullock as a sin offering for himself. But before taking its blood inside the tabernacle, he placed incense in a golden censer with live coals of fire and went behind the veil into the most holy place where the incense smoke covered over God's presence (Leviticus 16:12, 13). Failure to offer incense in this manner meant death for Aaron (Leviticus 16:13).

Third, Aaron took the blood of the young bullock and carried it behind the veil sprinkling it upon the mercy seat once and upon the east side of the ark of the covenant seven times (Leviticus 16:14). This sacrifice was for himself and the priests.

Fourth, after slaying the goat as a sin offering chosen by lot, he carried its blood behind the veil and sprinkled it upon the mercy seat and ark of the covenant in a similar manner as the bullock's blood. This completed the sin offering for the people. Simply standing there before the Lord accomplished his work. No ritual statement was necessary. It was enough that man was *there through the sacrifices.*[13] Then he took the blood of both the first and second animals and touched all articles of furniture for the cleansing of the tabernacle itself. Thus, a blood animal sacrifice had been offered to God for the sins of Aaron, the priesthood, the people, and for cleansing the tabernacle.

Fifth, upon the head of the scapegoat—the animal not chosen by lot—Aaron placed his hands and confessed the sins and transgressions of the people of Israel. An appointed man took the goat into the wilderness and left the animal there to die (Leviticus 16:21, 22).[14] Sixth, Aaron returned to the laver and, taking off the holy linen garments for this day of atonement, bathed a second time and dressed in his regular high priestly garments. Finally, he offered the two rams as burnt offerings for himself, the priests, and the people. (Leviticus 16:24).

Later in Jewish history, the ritual changed only in details. Its same meaning remained. The ritual is described in the Mishnah tractate *Yoma* as follows:[15]

> He came to his bullock and his bullock was standing between the Porch and the Altar, its head to the south and its face to the west; and he set both his hands upon it and made confession. And thus used he to say: "O God, I have committed iniquity, transgressed, and sinned before thee, I and my house. O God, forgive the iniquities and transgressions and sins which I have committed and transgressed and sinned before thee, I and my house, as it is written in the Law of thy servant Moses, for on this day shall atonement be made for you to cleanse you; from all your sins shall ye be clean before the Lord (Lev. 16:30)." And they answered after him, "Blessed be the name of the glory of his kingdom for ever and ever!" Yomah 3:8.

They brought out to him the ladle and the fire-pan and he took his two hands full [of incense] and put it on the ladle, which was large according to his largeness [of hand], or small according to his smallness [of hand]; and such [alone] was the prescribed measure of the ladle. He took the fire-pan in his right hand and the ladle in his left. He went through the Sanctuary until he came to the space between the two curtains separating the Sanctuary from the Holy of Holies. And there was a cubit's space between them. R. Jose says: Only one curtain was there, for it is written, And the veil shall divide for you between the holy place and the most holy (Exodus 26:33). The outer curtain was looped up on the south side and the inner one on the north side. He went along between them until he reached the north side; when he reached the north he turned round to the south and went on with the curtain on his left hand until he reached the Ark. When he reached the Ark he put the fire-pan between the two bars. He heaped up the incense on the coals and the whole place became filled with smoke. He came out by the way he went in, and in the outer space he prayed a short prayer. But he did not prolong his prayer lest he put Israel in terror.

After the Ark was taken away a stone remained there from the time of the early prophets, and it was called "Shetiyah." It was higher than the ground by three fingerbreadths. On this he used to put [the fire-pan].

He took the blood from him that was stirring it and entered [again] into the place where he had entered and stood [again] on the place whereon he had stood, and sprinkled [the blood] once upwards and seven times downwards, not as though he had intended to sprinkle upwards or downwards, but as though he were wielding a whip. And thus used he to count: One, one and one, one and two, one and three, one and four, one and five, one and six, one and seven. He came out and put it on the golden stand in the Sanctuary. Yoma 5.1 ff.

The two he-goats of the Day of Atonement should be alike in appearance, in size, and in value, and have been bought at the same time. Yet even if they are not alike they are valid. If one of them died before the lot was cast, a fellow may be bought for the other; but if after the lot was cast, another pair must be brought and the lots cast over them anew. And if that cast for the Lord died he [the high priest] should say, "Let this on which the lot 'For the Lord' has fallen stand in its stead"; and if that cast for Azazel died, he should say, "Let this on which the lot 'For Azazel' has fallen stand in its stead." The other is left to pasture until it suffers a blemish, when it must be sold and its value falls to the Temple fund; for the sin-offering of the congregation may not be left to die. R. Judah says: It is left to die. Moreover, R. Judah said: If the blood was poured away the scapegoat is left to die; if the scapegoat died, the blood is poured away.

He then came to the scapegoat and laid his two hands upon it and made confession. And thus used he to say: "O God, thy people, the House of Israel, have committed iniquity, transgressed, and sinned before thee. O God, forgive, I pray, the iniquities and transgressions and sins which thy people, the House of Israel have committed and transgressed and sinned before thee; as it is written in the Law of thy servant Moses, for on this day shall atonement be made for you to cleanse you; from all your sins shall ye be clean before the Lord (Leviticus 16:30). And when the priests and the people which stood in the Temple Court heard the Expressed Name come forth from the mouth of the High Priest, they used to kneel and bow themselves and fall down on their faces and say, "Blessed be the name of the glory of his kingdom for ever and ever!" Yoma 6:1 f.; 5:4-7.

On the Day of Atonement, eating, drinking, washing, anointing, putting on sandals, and marital intercourse are forbidden. A king or a bride may wash their faces and women after childbirth may put on sandals. So R. Eliezer. But the Sages forbit it. Yoma 8.1.

D. God's Reign

Another significant aspect of the Ark of the Covenant was its kingly meaning for the children of Israel. As a covenant people, Israel thought of Yahweh as her king. For Israel, Yahweh redeemed them from Egypt and declared,

> I am the Lord your God, who brought you out of the land of Egypt, out of the house of bondage. You shall have no other gods before me." Exodus 29:2, 3.

As a redeemed people, Israel owed its allegiance to Yahweh, not to the gods of other pagan religions that tempted them. Thus, their allegiance to Yahweh was in itself a political and spiritual act. Israel must separate itself from its neighbors and commit itself in obedience to Yahweh who ruled over them. Consequently, Israel thought of God as a King ruling among them with His throne at the Ark of the Covenant in the most holy place of the tabernacle.

Later in Israel's history the people requested a human king in an attempt to be like the other nations. This turn of events displeased the prophet Samuel and God.

> Then all the elders of Israel gathered together and came to Samuel at Ramah, and said to him, "Behold, you are old and your sons do not walk in your ways; now appoint for us a king to govern us like all the nations." But the thing displeased Samuel when they said, "Give us a king to govern us." And Samuel prayed to the Lord. And the Lord said to Samuel, "Hearken to the voice of the people in all that they say to you; for they have not rejected you, but they have rejected me from being king over them." 1 Samuel 8:4-7.

This move away from God as King to human kings led to the downfall of Israel as a nation. The biblical concept of the kingdom of God is the spiritual rule of God in the hearts of His people. It cannot be reduced to human politics and geographical borders. Unlike the pagan Syrian and Hittite views of their king, Israel's Ruler was invisible. Occasionally evidences of His presence could be seen, such as the cloud and pillar of fire, but God Himself stands beyond the visible and tangible. Newman says,

> If the ark was viewed as a throne, as far as the human eye could tell, it was an *empty* throne, upon which Yahweh was invisibly present. Thus it was the visible testimony to the invisible and continuing *presence* among the Hebrews of Yahweh, their God from Sinai.[16]

This concept of God's reign found expression in the use of cherubim over the mercy seat of the ark of the covenant.[17] The cherubim indicated the reign of God over His people. As part of the mercy seat of the ark of the covenant, mercy seat and cherubim combined as the place upon which Yahweh sat and reigned in the covenant community.[18] The law, of course, rested inside the ark of the covenant indicating that the law stood at the feet of the king. Thus, the ark of the covenant is sometimes called the throne of God (Jeremiah 3:16 f.) and God's footstool (1 Chronicles 28:2; Psalms 99:5; 132:7). Psalm 99:1 describes this important function of the ark and its cherubim in these words,

> The Lord reigns; let the peoples tremble! He sits enthroned upon the cherubim; let the earth quake!

As Israel's covenant God, Yahweh ruled not only over the people of Israel but the entire world. No other god was worthy of their attention. He who demolished the Egyptian gods by plagues, who delivered them from Egypt, now must be obeyed and submitted to as He ruled from the ark of the covenant in their midst. What a tragedy to reject this theocracy and turn to human kings with a geographical limitation to the concept of kingship!

God's reign in the midst of His people receives major attention in the New Testament. As early as Pentecost Jesus is called Lord, and His reign is described as fulfilling the prophecy of Joel and Psalm 110:1 (Acts 2:14-36). That reign is further affirmed by Stephen (Acts 7:44-50) and Paul (1 Corinthians 15:20-28; Ephesians 1:19-23; Colossians 1:15-20; Philippians 2:6-11). The New Testament views Christ as Lord ruling in the new kingdom. The church, as the new people of God, is described as the *ekklesia*, the people of God under the reign of Christ her Lord. There exists, therefore, a close tie between Israel under the rule of Yahweh as God's covenant people in the Old Testament and the church as God's new covenant people under the rule of its Lord (this title means the name Yahweh).

Crown Him with many crowns,
   The Lamb upon His throne;
Hark! how the heavenly anthem drowns
   All music but its own;
Awake, my soul, and sing
   Of Him who died for thee,
And hail Him as thy matchless King
   Through all eternity.

Crown Him the Lord of love:
   Behold His hands and side,
Rich wounds, yet visible above,
   In beauty glorified:
No angel in the sky
   Can fully bear that sight,
But downward bends his burning eye
   At mysteries so bright.

Crown Him the Lord of peace;
   Whose power a scepter sways
From pole to pole, that wars may cease,
   Absorbed in prayer and praise:
His reign shall know no end;
   And round His pierced feet
Fair flowers of paradise extend
   Their fragrance ever sweet.

Crown Him the Lord of years,
   The Potentate of time;
Creator of the rolling spheres,
   Ineffably sublime:
All hail, Redeemer, hail!
   For Thou hast died for me:
Thy praise shall never, never fail
   Throughout eternity.

—Matthew Bridges

6
PRIESTHOOD

Three great offices existed in the Old Testament: prophet, priest, and king. God was Israel's king during its early history. Later came human kings who reigned in the united monarchy, then in the Northern and Southern kingdoms of the divided monarchy. The kings ruled over the people as the function of kingship implies.

The prophets were spokesmen for God. They discerned the times and brought God's message to bear on the contemporary life of the children of Israel. They were primarily forthtellers of God's Word. During the united and divided monarchies, the prophets became the persons through whom the spiritual life of the people depended.

The priests represented the people to God. Whereas the prophet brought God's message to the people, the priests brought and represented the people before God.

Qualifications

Not everyone qualified for the priesthood. Special restrictions were placed upon the priests to preserve the integrity of this important function in Israel. Only Aaron and his sons and their descendants qualified for the priesthood.

The first qualification, therefore, to be a priest was proof of one's line of descent from Aaron. However, some exceptions to this rule came about as in the case of Samuel who discharged some priestly duties (1 Samuel 2:18 f.; 1 Samuel 9:11-13; 13:5-15) even though he was an Ephramite (1 Samuel 1:1). And in some places Levites functioned as priests as we learn from Judges 17:7-13.

A second qualification for the priesthood is that one needed to be without blemish. Even if one traced his ancestry back to Aaron, he must pass the test of holiness as set forth in the following passage.

> And the Lord said to Moses, "Say to Aaron, None of your descendants throughout their generations who has a blemish may approach to offer the bread of his God. For no one who has a blemish shall draw near, a man blind or lame, or one who has a mutilated face or a limb too long, or a man who has an injured foot or an injured hand, or a hunchback, or a dwarf, or a man with a defect in his sight or an itching disease or scabs or crushed testicles; no man of the descendants of Aaron the priest who has a blemish shall come near to offer the Lord's offerings by fire; since he has a blemish, he shall not come near to offer the bread of his God. He may eat the bread of his God, both of the most holy and of the holy things, but he shall not come near the veil or approach the altar, because he has a blemish, that he may not profane my sanctuaries; for I am the Lord who sanctify them." Leviticus 21:16-23.

The priests were allowed to marry, but special regulations guided the high priest in regard to whom he chose as his wife. She must be a virgin from his own people. A widow, divorcee, defiled lady, and a harlot were disqualified from becoming the wife of the high priest (Leviticus 21:13, 14).

Consecration

A special consecration took place when the priests were anointed for their duties and began their work. The consecration act required one young bull, two rams without blemish, unleavened bread, unleavened cakes mixed with oil, and unleavened wafers spread with oil. These baked goods consisted of fine wheat flour (Exodus 29:1, 2).

After dressing in special priestly garments the anointing oil was poured upon the head of each individual priest (Exodus 29:7).

After the young bull was brought before the group and after placing hands upon its head, it was slain and its blood placed upon the horns of the brazen altar. Any remaining blood was poured out at the base of the altar (Exodus 29:10-12).

The blood of one ram was thrown against the brazen altar on each of its four sides (Exodus 29:15, 16).

Finally, the second ram, when slain, had its blood placed upon the tip of the right ear of each priest, upon the thumb of each priest's right hand, and upon the big toe of the right foot of each priest. The remainder of the blood was then thrown against the altar (Exodus 29:19, 20).

The wheat cakes, wafers, and unleavened bread with other parts of the rams were waved before the Lord as a wave offering (Exodus 29:22-25), after which they burned upon the brazen altar as a burnt offering. The high priest's consecration took place in a similar way.

In this act of consecration, the priests found themselves set apart for God's holy service. Instead of being incapacitated by amputation, these priests and their bodily limbs now were consecrated to do God's work. The ear was touched with blood in order that it might be consecrated to hear and be sensitive to the law of God. The thumb was touched with blood in order that it might be consecrated to perform the duties of the priesthood, including offering the sacrifices to God. And the toe was covered with blood in order that the foot might walk in the path of righteousness and show the way for the people to come to God.

To be a priest in Israel was as great a task as being prophet. In contrast to the prophetic role, the priestly function implied listening instead of talking, compassion instead of criticism, and bearing the people's sins in God's presence for forgiveness instead of merely pointing them out.

Duties

The priestly role first implied the concept of *representation.* Priests carried the responsibility of representing the people before God. Second, the priestly role implied the principle of *intercession.* As the persons who carried the major task of sacrificing before God, the priests interceded for the people. Therefore, the duties of the priesthood were strictly religious and centered around the work of sacrifices at the tabernacle and later the temple. They did not hold political office nor did they have any political power. Their services, means of fiscal support by the people, and food came by way of the free gifts of the people including the tithe.

Priests did not become a special caste of people, nor a hierarchy. Rather priests accepted their divinely appointed responsibility as a medium of communication between the people and God.

While specific duties varied from time to time and from priest to priest, their main activities included:

1. Helping the people in offering the sacrifices.
2. Caring for and lighting the lamps on the lampstand.
3. Changing the shewbread on the table every week.
4. Offering incense at the incense altar.
5. Preparing the tabernacle furniture for moving.

Obviously, their main work related to sacrifices. Here the

priest actually carried out the sacrificial ritual in many of the sacrifices, though not all, and thereby stood between the people and God in the act of worship. Because of their sin the people could not achieve a personal, experiential relationship with God. Both a priest as mediator and an animal as a sacrifice were required before divine fellowship between the people and God actually happened.

On a normal day the priests arose early in the morning in response to a call by the Levites. They washed hands and feet at the laver, removed the ashes from the brazen altar, and piled fresh wood on the altar, to be consumed by fire during the day. They carefully arranged any sacrificial remnants on the altar from the preceding evening's sacrifices. Thus at the dawn of the new day the altar was already prepared for its work.

Then, as one priest sacrificed the lamb as a burnt offering, including the proper sacrificial use of its blood, another replenished the oil in the lampstand. And while the fire began to consume the offering at the altar in the courtyard, the incense smoke began to rise from the incense altar. As the fragrance of these sacrifices began ascending toward God, the people gathered near the gate of the courtyard and the presiding priest came out of the tabernacle and walked toward the people. With hands uplifted he pronounced the sacred benediction,

> The Lord bless you and keep you:
> The Lord make his face to shine upon you,
> And be gracious to you:
> The Lord lift up his countenance upon you,
> and give you peace. Numbers 6:24-26.

High Priest

The priestly office reached its highest development in the

high priest. God chose Aaron, brother of Moses, to carry out this holy function. He represented the people before God on the great day of atonement by placing the blood of the sacrifice upon the mercy seat of the ark of the covenant. So important was the role of the high priest that it followed, by God's choice, the family line of Aaron. This high priest passed from son to son throughout the generations. Aaron himself was anointed and consecrated as high priest over Israel at God's command by Moses (Leviticus 8:1-13). His sons, Nadab, Abihu, Eleazer, and Ithamar then stood in line to become high priests.

However, the disobedience of Nadab and Abihu, in which they offered an incense offering with strange fire rather than the fire from the brazen altar, brought God's wrath in the form of a fire that devoured them and they died (Leviticus 10:1, 2). Only Eleazer and Ithamar were left to take up the high priestly office.

Only one direct male descendant of Aaron held the office of high priest at one time. According to Josephus, more than eighty men officiated in this capacity between Aaron and Christ.[1] The only reason for changing from one high priest to another was the death of the former. Not always, however, did this method of becoming high priest hold in Israel's later history. During the intertestamental period and the first century CE other ways were found to appoint the high priest. For example, Bruce has found that,

> After the deposition of Onias II in 174 BC, Jason and later Menelaus were appointed to the high priesthood by Antiochus IV; Alcimus was appointed by Demetrius I in 162 BC; the Hasmonean Jonathan was appointed by Alexander Balas, putative son of Antiochus IV, in 152 BC, his brother Simon and his successors were appointed by decree of the Jewish people in 140 BC (1 Maccabees 14:41). With the fall of the Hasmonean

> house the high priests were appointed successively by Herod the Great (37-4 BC), Archelaus (4 BC-AD 6), Roman governors (AD 6-41), and members of the Herod family (AD 41-66). The last high priest, Phanni, son of Samuel, was appointed by popular ballot during the war against Rome (c. AD 67).[2]

As high priest, Aaron was consecrated in a similar manner as the other priests, but his role carried more significance, symbolized by the difference in garments which he wore from those of the regular priests.

Garments

The priesthood expressed itself with three sets of garments; the garments for the ordinary priests, the high priestly garments worn through the year, and the special linen garment made for and worn only on the day of atonement by the high priest.

Ordinary priests wore four garments: white linen breeches, a tunic of white linen, an embroidered girdle, and a white head gear.

The high priest wore three additional garments. The garments, of course, distinguished the priests from the people and the high priest from the other priests. Thus, the garments symbolized the gradation of holiness among Israel. But the garments themselves did not make the priests holy. Instead the garments reminded the priests and the high priest of the holiness to which God called them. In other words, priestly garments did not symbolize the holy character of the priest, rather it set forth symbolically the degree of holiness that should have characterized his life according to the law. These garments, therefore, actually became a reminder of what the priest's character should have been, but was not. As Hirsch writes,

> it is just in clothing himself for the service of the Sanctuary in these priestly garments that he expresses to himself and to others his own real imperfection.[3]

High priestly garments consisted of the following (see Fig. 21). First, the breeches or trousers were made of white linen and worn for the purpose of modesty while tending the brazen altar. In contrast to pagan religions in which the act of worship involved a sexual rite, the Hebrew and Christian worship in purity of heart before God. Slemming says,

> Much of the idol worship was sensual, sexual, obscene, and nakedness was often part of their conduct. For the worshipper of God there must be modesty and decency, for we must worship Him in the beauty of holiness.[4]

Second, the tunic of white linen was put over the head and fastened at the neck. This tunic extended all the way to the ground upon which the priest stood, thereby covering the entire body.

Third, over the tunic lay a blue robe (Exodus 28:31-35; 38:22-26) which, according to Haran, was of *oreg* workmanship.[5] This robe was woven with twelve strands of blue thread and covered the body, except for the arms and head, all the way down to six inches above the ground.[6] At the bottom of this blue robe pomegranates, a fruit in the Near East, were sewn. Between each pomegranate was a bell. As the high priest walked, these bells rang as they bumped into the pomegranates, thereby indicating to the assembled Israelites that the high priest was alive and well in the midst of his duties in the holy place.[7]

Fourth, came the ephod, an apronlike garment with straps over each shoulder (Exodus 28:6-14; 27; 39:2-7, 20). Haran describes this woven fabric as follows:

Fig. 21. The High Priest and Garments

1. Tunic

2. Robe

3. Bells and Pomegranates

4. Ephod

5. Belt or Girdle

6. Breastplate

7. Miter

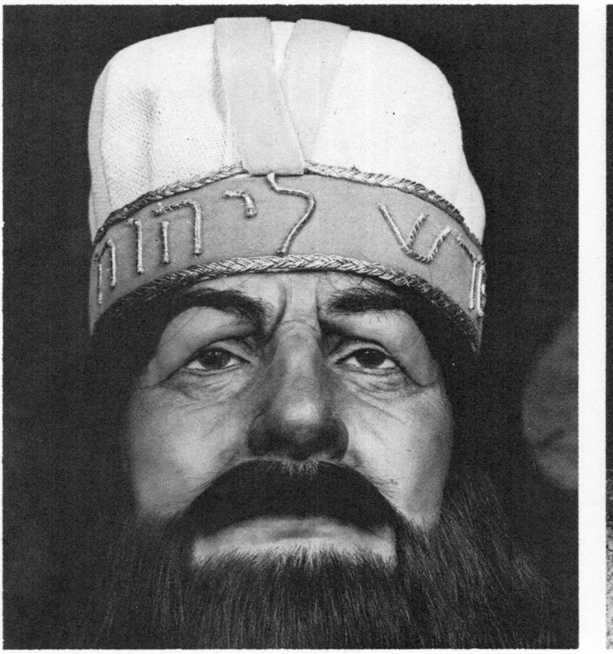

8. Fully Dressed

> The ephod is made of the sacred mixture—all kinds of wool with linen, *hoshev* workmanship, and from this aspect it seems to be similar to the *parokheth*-veil of the lower curtains. Nevertheless, it differs in some important details from the latter. First, no figures of cherubim are mentioned, though it is made according to *hoshev* workmanship. Presumably there are really no figures of cherubim, but only designs of a general nature adorned thereon. Second, in the ephod gold is woven, in addition to the threads of wool and linen. What is more, gold becomes the predominant element, outstripping in quantity all the other elements woven into this fabric. This is indicated, above all, by the fact that in the list of materials used in the ephod, gold is mentioned first and only afterwards blue, purple, crimson stuff, and linen.[8]

Upon the straps over the shoulders of the high priest an onyx stone lay into which the names of the children of Israel were engraved. These stones (one on each shoulder) each had six names of the children of Israel engraved therein "in the order of their birth" (Exodus 28:10). This means that Reuben, Simeon, Levi, Judah, Dan, and Naphtali were engraved in one stone and Gad, Asher, Issachar, Zebulon, Joseph, and Benjamin were engraved in the other stone. These stones symbolized that the high priest, as mediator for the people, carried the very weight of their sin upon his shoulders. As high priest he bore the spiritual life of the people upon himself when acting as mediator between God and them.[9]

Fifth, a belt or girdle, woven like the ephod and about 6 inches wide, went around the middle of the high priest and was tied in front thereby keeping the ephod tight to his body.

Sixth, a breastplate covered over the breast of the high priest and laid in front of the ephod (see Fig. 22). Woven similar to the ephod it measured eighteen inches long and nine inches wide. When folded in the middle it became

Fig. 22. The Breastplate and Stones

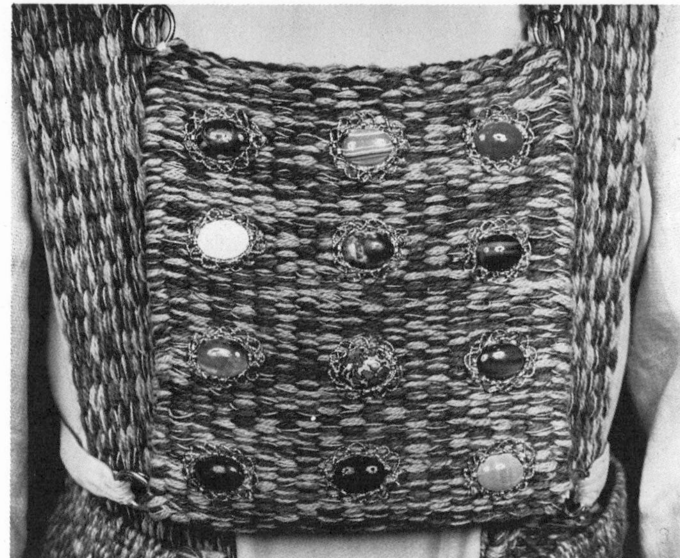

square with an inside pocket as a storage place for the Urim and Thummim, objects by which the high priest discerned the will of God at times. This breastplate was fastened by six rings, two chains, and two frames. Two of these rings were fastened at the mid part of the ephod, two were fastened at the lower edge, and two were fastened at the top corners. A blue band ran through the rings on the bottom edge and around the back of the high priest where it tied. On the top part of the breastplate two golden chains ran from the rings to the shoulders of the high priest where they fastened to the two frames or settings upon which the onyx stones were placed in the straps of the ephod (Exodus 28:22-28; 39:15-21).

Twelve stones rested upon the breastplate representing each of the twelve tribes of Israel (see Fig. 22). Each stone

Fig. 23. Biblical and Modern Stones for the Breastplate

HEBREW NAME		STONE NAME	ORDER BY BIRTH	ORDER BY CAMP	MODERN STONE NAME
		Row 1			
1. Odem	אֹדֶם	Sardus	Reuben	Judah	Sard
2. Pitdah	פִּטְדָה	Topaz	Simeon	Issachar	Peridot
3. Baraketh	בָּרֶקֶת	Emerald	Levi	Zebulon	Malachite
		Row 2			
4. Nophek	נֹפֶךְ	Carbuncle	Judah	Reuben	Garnet
5. Sapphire	סַפִּיר	Sapphire	Dan	Simeon	Lapis Lazuli
6. Yahalom	יַהֲלֹם	Diamond	Naphtali	Gad	Corundum
		Row 3			
7. Leshem	לֶשֶׁם	Ligure	Gad	Ephraim	Amber
8. Shebo	שְׁבוֹ	Agate	Assher	Manasseh	Agate
9. Ahlamah	אַחְלָמָה	Amethyst	Issachar	Benjamin	Amethyst
		Row 4			
10. Tarshis	תַּרְשִׁישׁ	Beryl	Zebulon	Dan	Beryl
11. Sholom	שֹׁהַם	Onyx	Joseph	Assher	Quartz
12. Yashpheh	יָשְׁפֵה	Jasper	Benjamin	Naphtali	Jasper

was carefully chosen as a representation of the character of a given tribe and its leader and, therefore, became "stones of remembrance for the sons of Israel" (Exodus 28:12; 39:7).

These stones were arranged in four rows with three stones in each row according to the order given in Exodus 28:17-21 and 39:10-14. Of course, the stones appeared in the order of the Hebrew text which moved from right to left in the arrangement.

The order of the stones given in the Hebrew text and their equivalent today are shown in Fig. 23.[10]

These stones served as a continual reminder to Aaron that not only did he represent the people and act as their intercessor by bearing their weight on his shoulders, but that as high priest he must constantly keep himself close to the people and the people close to himself. Thus, the stones over his heart indicated his role of exercising compassion and tender love toward them.

> So Aaron shall bear the names of the sons of Israel in the breastpiece of judgment upon his heart, when he goes into the holy place, to bring them to continual remembrance before the Lord. Exodus 28:29.

Within the pocket of the breastplate rested the Urim and Thummim (Exodus 28:30). Many ideas have emerged as to what kind of objects these were; sticks of wood, the twelve stones of the breastplate, lights, four extra letters of the Hebrew alphabet, etc. Perhaps it is best to admit that we do not know what kind of objects they were.

But their purpose is clear. The high priest used them to determine the will of God. At times of doubt or national crisis, the Urim and Thummim were consulted (Numbers 27:21; 1 Samuel 28:6). The manner in which the high priest used them is not clear. A clear "aye" or "no" answer came forth, however, when they were used to inquire about the will of God (1 Samuel 14:41 ff.).

After the days of David, there is no mention of these objects indicating, perhaps, that the prophets then became the spokesman for God and no other means was necessary, whereas earlier in Israel's history, during the period of the wilderness, the conquest, and the judges, there was need to consult the Urim and Thummim to discern the will of God.

Seventh, a headgear for the high priest, called the mitre (Exodus 28:36-38; 39:28, 30), lay upon his head. It was a piece of linen woven around his head several times. While the headgear of the regular priest, as well as the high priest, wrapped around the head, they were not wrapped in the same manner. The length of the band was 16 cubits for both. Across the front of the headgear, from ear to ear, a golden plate was fastened, two fingers wide, upon which were written the words *kodesh la Yahweh,* or in English,

Holiness to the Lord.[11] This golden plate was kept in place by a blue band which tied at the back of the head.

All of these garments gave the high priest a beautiful appearance. That is precisely why his garments were given, for glory and for beauty (Exodus 28:2).

On the day of atonement, as already noted, the high priest changed his garments and dressed in all white (Leviticus 16:4). These white garments, used only on this one day of the year, signified the holy character of his work. They further signified that he did not appear in glory and beauty on this day, but in soberness and seriousness. Only when the sins of the people were dealt with in God's holy presence did the high priest again dress in his garments of glory and beauty.

As we will note later in this book, Christ fulfilled the high priestly role. He fully represented humankind before God in His sacrificial atoning work.

Five bleeding wounds He bears,
   Received on Calvary;
They pour effectual prayers,
   They strongly speak for me;
Forgive him, O forgive, they cry,
   Forgive him, O forgive, they cry,
Nor let the ransomed sinner die!

He ever lives above
   For me to intercede,
His all redeeming love,
   His precious blood to plead;
His blood atoned for all our race,
   His blood atoned for all our race,
And sprinkles now the throne of grace.
—Charles Wesley

7
MOVEMENT AND HISTORY OF THE TABERNACLE

As already observed, the tabernacle was constructed so that it could easily be dismantled and moved. Movement from one encampment to the next is a fascinating story. In this story one discovers the orderliness and care by which Israel protected the tabernacle.

Moving the Tabernacle

Most of the work involved in transporting the tabernacle was given to the Levites. The tribe of Levi was divided among his three sons, Gershon, Kohath, and Merari, who were born to Levi in Canaan and went down into Egypt with the other children of Israel (Genesis 46:11). These male descendants of Levi's three sons received appointment to protect the tabernacle and to move it during the wilderness journey (Numbers 1:50). They must not touch the sacred articles of furniture lest they die (Numbers 4:15). The Levites distinguished themselves from the priests in that the priests cleaned the sacred vessels of the tabernacle and prepared them for moving, whereas, the Levites assumed responsibility for protecting the tabernacle and moving it. To do so, a special rite of purification was required (Numbers 8:1-22). A Levite became eligible for service at a minimum of 25 years of age and they retired at 50 years of age.[1]

In the encampment a special orderly arrangement existed for the tribes. On the east, nearest to the courtyard, Moses, Aaron, and the priests lived (Numbers 3:38). The Levites assigned living area was also nearest to the courtyard with the Kohathites on the south (Numbers 3:29), Merarites on the north (Numbers 3:35), and Gershonites on the west (Numbers 3:23). They numbered a total of 8,580 men between the ages of thirty and fifty (Numbers 4:46-49). The inner circle of priests and Levites were given the responsibility to care for the tabernacle and carry out its operation.

Beyond this inner core the twelve tribes encamped. On the east Judah, Issachar, and Zebulun encamped for protection (Numbers 2:2-10); on the south, Reuben, Simeon, and Gad (Numbers 2:10-16); on the west, Ephraim, Benjamin, and Manasseh (Numbers 2:18-24); and on the north, Dan, Naphtali, and Asher (Numbers 2:25-31).

God's presence found symbolic expression by the cloud hovering over the tabernacle during the day and a pillar of fire at night. When the cloud began to move, indicating God's leading forward to the next encampment, the silver trumpet blew and the whole camp went into action in the moving process (Numbers 10:4, 5). The tribes on the east side moved in the direction that the cloud moved. While these eastern tribes moved, the inner circle of priests began preparing the articles of furniture for moving. Aaron and his sons covered the ark of the covenant with the veil *(parokheth)* (Numbers 4:5).[2] Upon this veil the priests next placed a covering of *tahash* and a final covering of blue (Numbers 4:6). In fact, each article of furniture in the tabernacle was covered by the priests before the Levites moved them (Numbers 4:1-16).

- The incense altar was covered with a blue cloth and by a second covering of *tahash* skins.
- The utensils on the table of shewbread were wrapped in a blue cloth, then a covering of scarlet laid over the table and the utensils, and finally a covering of *tahash* skins over the top.
- The utensils at the lampstand were wrapped up in a blue cloth, the lampstand and utensils covered with a blue cloth, and a covering of *tahash* skins over the top. The lampstand was placed in a special carrying frame since no staves fastened to it.
- Scripture is silent regarding how the laver was covered and moved;
- After ashes were removed the brazen altar utensils were covered with a purple covering and a covering of *tahash* skins over the top.

Aaron's son, Eleazer, held responsibility for taking care of the oil for the lampstand, the incense for the incense altar, the cereal offering, and the anointing oil (Numbers 4:16).

When the priests finished preparing the articles of furniture for moving, the Kohathites entered the tabernacle. After placing staves in the articles of furniture, they carried each piece of furniture on their shoulders to a designated place outside of the courtyard as the eastern tribes moved in the direction God led them. The Kohathites held these upon their shoulders perhaps until the remainder of the tabernacle was dismantled and carried past them by the Gershonites and Merarites.

The Gershonites carefully removed the four coverings from the top of the tabernacle, the screen at the door, the curtain around the courtyard and, under the supervision of Ithamar, placed these upon two wagons pulled by four oxen (Numbers 4:28; 7:7).

Immediately, the Merarites took down the bars, boards, and pillars in the tabernacle and the courtyard with their accompanying pegs, cords, and bases. They placed them upon four wagons pulled with eight oxen under the approving eye of Ithamar (Numbers 4:29-33; 7:8).

Thereupon, the Gershonites, followed by the Merarites, with oxen pulling wagons containing the tabernacle materials, marched behind the camp of Judah.

With the head of the march moving, Moses blew the second trumpet (Numbers 10:6) and the camps of Reuben, Simeon, and Gad moved into the line of march from the south side of the tabernacle. These three tribes were then followed by the Kohathites carrying the articles of furniture on their shoulders (Numbers 7:9). Apparently the ark of the covenant was actually at the front of the line of march under the protection of the holy cloud (Numbers 10:33, 34).

These Kohathites were followed by the tribes of Ephraim, Benjamin, and Manasseh from the west and finally the tribes of Dan, Naphtali, and Asher from the north who acted as a rear guard for all the tribes and tabernacle (Numbers 10:25).

Thus, the camp of Judah marched right behind the ark of the covenant to protect it, the Kohathites marched in the middle of the line with the sacred articles of furniture, and the camp of Dan provided protection from the rear. As the total camp moved forward in this orderly procession, Moses cried out:

> Arise, O Lord, and let thy enemies be scattered; and let them that hate thee flee before thee. Numbers 10:35.

Upon the arrival at the next place of encampment the holy cloud rested upon the ark of the covenant. The tribe of Judah marched past the ark and waited on the east side to protect it while the Gershonites and Merarites erected the tabernacle once more.

As the camp of Reuben arrived, it marched to the south side of the encampment along with the other two tribes on the south. The Kohathites carried the articles of furniture inside the newly erected tabernacle and placed them in their designated spot. Obviously, the Kohathites did not wait upon other Levites since the tabernacle building was already erected when they arrived. Immediately thereafter the camps of Ephraim and Dan, with the other tribes, filled in the west and north sides of the encampment.

Finally, the priests uncovered the articles of furniture and, after carrying the ark of the covenant to the most holy place, they removed its coverings including the veil. Without looking at the ark of the covenant, they raised the veil into its proper position and hung it on the pillars.

In this orderly and simple way the tabernacle was moved from encampment to encampment during the wilderness journey. Obviously, not all questions are answered regarding the moving of the tabernacle. For example, we do not know how long it took to move (perhaps two hours?). Another question arises regarding weight. Could the tabernacle be hauled by twelve oxen pulling six wagons? We must admit that we do not know the size of the wagons nor the size of the oxen.

Without discrediting these questions, please permit the present writer to clarify that the biblical narrative's intention shows the reader that God led and took care of His people during the wilderness journey. The purpose of the narrative is not to describe who tightened each screw or whether the Levites turned the screw driver with the right hand or the left hand! Rather, the biblical narrative focuses the reader's attention upon the most important matters with an orderly and simple explanation of the movement of the tabernacle in the line of march.

History of the Tabernacle and Ark of the Covenant

Literary studies of the Pentateuch indicate that the first five books of Moses were put together in literary sections or documents identified as J, E, D, P (see Appendix). In these literary documents one finds two shrine traditions; one dealing with the ark of the covenant in the E document and the other dealing with the "tent of meeting" in the J document. While the older Graft-Wellhausen view of these documents is no longer held by most Old Testament scholars, the idea of documents is generally accepted.

Newman, for example, finds through his literary studies two early traditions concerning the covenant at Mt. Sinai. From here he perceives also early traditions regarding two important shrines at Mt. Sinai. Thus he concludes that both the ark of the covenant and the tent of meeting appear first at Mt. Sinai.[3] According to this view, the ark of the covenant and the tent of meeting were separate entities until the children of Israel entered into the Promised Land. They were united when the tent of meeting became the tabernacle and the ark of the covenant was placed inside of it at Shiloh. During the period leading up to this union, the tent existed in the north and the ark of the covenant in the south moving to Shechem, Gilgal, Shiloh, and Jerusalem.[4]

Later, according to this view, the P document was written by the priests around the time of the Exile. This document strongly emphasized the tabernacle, describing it in detail (Exodus 25—31, 35—40), to clarify from Israel's earlier history that God cannot be confined to the temple at Jerusalem. God is a moving and acting God among His people wherever they exist.

Contrary to the old Graft-Wellhausen view, the P document is not a pious fraud formed by the priests regarding the tabernacle, but is based on important oral tradition handed down by the children of Israel from the time the tabernacle first arose until it was written. Frank M. Cross says,

> In the last analysis, it can in no way represent pious fraud, but rather the best efforts of priestly scholars who tried to piece together the golden past from materials available to them.[5]

Thus, even if one follows the documentary view of the Pentateuch, he is led to the conclusion that from its earliest beginnings at Sinai Israel had a central sanctuary as the center for its worship life. Kraus says,

> We know today that the Israelite tribal confederacy possessed right from the beginning one institution of a central sanctuary as the basis of its cultic life.[6]

If, however, one rejects the documentary view, it is possible to interpret the "tent of meeting" as a shrine where God met Moses prior to the building of the tabernacle (Exodus 33:7-11) and the tabernacle as the building described in Exodus 25—31 and 35—40 in the Sinai setting. Either literary view of the Pentateuch leads to the same conclusion, namely, that Israel's ark of the covenant and tent of meeting were, as de Vaux says, "part and parcel of the worship in the desert."[7] And if we disregard literary criticism, one concludes that the entire tabernacle structure was built and used during the wilderness period.

At the Sinai setting the covenant was formed (Exodus 19—24), the law was given to regulate the life of the covenant people (Exodus 20), and the tabernacle constructed as a means by which God dwelt in the midst of

His people in His theocratic rule over them with their response of worship through the sacrifices. In obedience to God, the tabernacle was erected on the first day of the first month of the second year after the departure from Egypt (Exodus 40:17).[8]

It was set up, taken down, moved, and erected again as they traveled through the wilderness. Numbers 33 lists the places of encampment from the time they left Egypt until they crossed the Jordan River and entered the promised land. At least 30 places of encampment are given between Mt. Sinai and the crossing of the Jordan. Chief of these places is Kadesh-barnea where they rested for some time while the spies went into the land. Two spies returned with good reports and the remaining ten spies came with negative reports. Consequently, of all the men who came out of Egypt only Caleb and Joshua entered the promised land (Numbers 14:30).

Crossing the Jordan became an exciting experience to say the least. During the wilderness journey, the ark of the covenant led the way to the next place of encampment. Now at the Jordan it led the way through this body of water. According to Joshua 3, the Levites first stepped into the water carrying the ark of the covenant. Then while standing in midstream holding the ark, all of Israel passed by, including those who carried the tabernacle.

After crossing the Jordan, they encamped at Gilgal for fourteen years during the conquest of the land (Joshua 7:6). During the miraculous raid upon the city of Jericho, the ark of the covenant set forth God's presence and power among the Israelites and had a direct bearing on the fall of that city. From here they encamped at Bethel (Judges 20:27). Finally, the tabernacle stood at Shiloh where it remained for 369 years.[9]

While at Shiloh during the days of Samuel, the ark of the covenant was removed from the most holy place and used in battle against the Philistines in the battle at Apheq where the Philistines captured it (1 Samuel 4:3, 11). It was taken to Ashdod and placed in the house of the pagan Philistine god, Dagan. The next morning the Philistines discovered that Dagan had fallen face downward before the ark of the covenant (1 Samuel 5:3). The very next day the same thing happened until the limbs of the pagan idol Dagan had fallen off. Because the ark of the covenant created difficulties for this pagan religion, it was taken to Gath (1 Samuel 5:8). After creating a plague upon the people of the city, the ark was taken to Ekron (1 Samuel 5:10). Here it created no small stir among the Philistine people as they cried out,

> They have brought around to us the ark of the God of Israel to slay us and our people. . . . Send away the ark of the God of Israel, and let it return to its own place, that it may not slay us and our people (1 Samuel 5:10, 11).

After holding the ark for seven months (1 Samuel 6:1), the Philistines returned it to the Israelites upon a cart pulled by two cows who went straight to Bethshemesh "lowing as they went" (1 Samuel 6:10-16).

Once the Israelites possessed the Ark again, they took it to Kiriath-jearim where it remained for twenty years or longer (1 Samuel 7:1).

Then the tabernacle and the ark of the covenant were moved from Shiloh to Nob, where David ate the shewbread (1 Samuel 21:1-6). Then it was taken to Gibeon (1 Kings 3:1-5; 2 Chronicles 5:2). Together, these two places kept the tabernacle in their midst for 57 years.

During this time the ark of the covenant was taken out of the old tabernacle and transported to Jerusalem on a cart drawn by oxen. Along the way one ox stumbled and Uzza, a willing helper, laid his hand on the ark of the covenant to prevent it from tumbling off. Though Uzza had done a heroic act, he had broken the law and died immediately (2 Samuel 6:6-8). Due to this tragic event, the ark was kept at the house of Obed-edom for three months. Then the Levites transported it to Jerusalem, carrying it in the manner prescribed in the law, and placed it "inside the tent" which David had built for it.[10] Whether this was a new tabernacle or the old one with new coverings, we cannot be sure. Psalm 132 describes this joyous occasion.

Later Solomon built a temple and placed the ark of the covenant and some of the articles of furniture from the tabernacle in it (1 Kings 8:1-9; 2 Chronicles 5:2-10). Strong writes,

> The candelabrum, however, if still extant was replaced, in this edifice, by ten others, probably of a more gorgeous style (1 Kings 7:49), with at least a repeating of the altar of incense and the table of shewbread (1 Kings 7:48). The laver, having probably long since been broken up, was also magnificently replaced (1 Kings 7:23, 27).[11]

By now, of course, the coverings over the top of the ancient tabernacle decayed and the boards and pillars were no longer useful. So with the building of the temple, the tabernacle, as such, came to an end. However, the ark of the covenant was placed in the new temple where it rested until 587 BC when Nebuchadnezzar's army destroyed the temple and wrecked the articles of furniture.

As far as we know, the destruction of the temple in 587 BC marked the end of the ark of the covenant. Josephus clearly states that it was not found in the second temple and the growth of speculation regarding its whereabouts indicates that it no longer existed.[12] We are safe in concluding from Jeremiah 3:16 and the Rabbinic literature that its destruction came with the fall of the temple in 587 BC. The Mishnah tractate *Yoma* reads:

> After the Ark was taken away, a stone remained there from the time of the early prophets, and it was called "Shetiyah." Yoma 5:20.[13]

From this intertestamental and Rabbinical information we cannot, therefore, accept a view held by the Coptic Church that it exists today in Ethiopia.

Thus, the tabernacle ended and with it the ark of the covenant, Israel's most sacred article of furniture. By AD 70 the sacrifices also ended with the destruction of the second temple.

Must we conclude that these precious parts of Israel's spiritual life ended in vain? Was the destruction of the temple and the ark of the covenant the end? The answer is an emphatic "no." A new chapter of the story arises! A new people come forth with a new covenant, a new sacrifice, and a new temple! For these, we turn to the New Testament fulfillment of what the tabernacle symbolized and promised.

The Lord is King, O praise His name,
  O'er all the earth His grace proclaim!
From age to age, from day to day,
  His wonders grow more gloriously.

O see the mighty hand of God,
  His love and mercy changeth not!
His blood and righteousness avail;
  His grace and pardon never fail!

—Nocolaus Ludwig von Zinzendorf
(translated by Esther Bergen)

8
CHRIST THE RECONCILER

A forward look toward the New Testament and its explanation of the tabernacle has emerged in the preceding pages. In this chapter the formation of a new covenant people will be examined on the basis of God's fullness of revelation. What the Old Testament promised and what the tabernacle symbolized now come to fulfillment in the New Testament in Christ and His church. A study of the tabernacle is not complete without examining its fulfillment.

The Need for Reconciliation

Redemption was not complete in the Old Testament. Though Israel experienced deliverance from Egypt and committed itself to a covenant with God, something was missing. Sin continued among the Israelites.

For example, at Sinai they became guilty of idolatry by worshiping a golden calf. So disgusted did Moses become that he threw the tables of the law and broke them in pieces (Exodus 32:19, 20), begged for God's pardon (Exodus 32:31-34), and witnessed the plague which God placed upon the people because of their disobedience (Exodus 32:35). During the wilderness journey sin expressed itself in many ways. They murmured because of their diet and God smote the people with a great plague at Kibroth-hattaavah (Numbers 11). Miriam was struck with leprosy because she spoke evil of Moses (Numbers 12). At Kadesh, rather than moving forward in faith and entering the land, they listened to a false report from ten spies and murmured against God. Consequently, God did not allow them to enter into the promised land. All who came out of Egypt, except Caleb and Joshua, died amidst their wanderings in the wilderness before crossing the Jordan River (Numbers 13, 14).

Amidst their disobedience, the children of Israel discovered God is holy and cannot tolerate sin. On one hand, at the tabernacle Israel learned that God desired to dwell among His people, but on the other hand Israel learned that, due to God's holiness and their sinfulness, God was separated from the people. God's holiness is clearly set forth in the Old Testament tabernacle. The idea of holiness is discovered in the term *Kodesh,* which means to be aloft or separated from sin. That which is holy is set aside from the unclean and unholy and consecrated to God's service.

In the tabernacle evidence abounds of God's holiness and humankind's sinfulness and the resultant separation between the two. First, nothing unholy was allowed within the camp (Leviticus 13:46), defiled persons were excluded (Deuteronomy 23:10), and the ashes from the sacrifices were carried outside the camp and burned (Leviticus 4:11, 12).

A second mark of separation is the placement of the people. An obvious gradation existed beginning with Aaron the high priest who could enter into the most holy place only on the Day of Atonement. Next came the priests and Levites who entered the holy place and the courtyard but could not enter the most holy place. Outside the fence of the courtyard were the Levites. Beyond them the Israelite families arranged in camps by tribes. Finally out beyond them all and furthest from God were the non-Jewish people. This gradation in arranging the people clearly sets forth God's holiness.

Third, one discovers gradations in the materials used for constructing the tabernacle. Closest to God stood the ark of the covenant with its pure and refined gold mercy seat. In the holy place stood the altar of incense, table of shewbread, and golden lampstand. Whereas, the mercy seat at the ark of the covenant consisted of *pure gold*, the table of shewbread had gold *laid over* the wood, and the lampstand was *beaten gold*. When one gets to the courtyard, the metal is copper—much less valuable than gold. How these articles of furniture were covered during the movement from one encampment to the next clearly shows the differing value.

Fourth, a gradation in tabernacle fabrics is also observed. The type of threads used in the fabrics indicated their value. Haran says,

> Three dyed wools are mentioned as ingredients in the work of weaving: blue, purple, and crimson. There should be no doubt that the text lists these varieties in their order of importance. Blue is accordingly regarded as the most expensive, purple slightly less, crimson less still.[1]

In addition to the thread colors three kinds of workmanship in descending order are found in the tabernacle fabrics. In the veil *(paroketh)* superior workmanship called *hoshev* is employed which included weaving cherubim in the fabric and beginning the weave with the blue yarn followed by the other colors. The first of four coverings over the top *(mishkan)* also employed superior workmanship *(hoshev)*, meaning that cherubim were woven into it, but here the weave began with white linen rather than blue, thus depicting a fabric of slightly less value than the veil. Then came the screen *(masak)* at the door of the tabernacle implying *roqem* workmanship, meaning that no cherubim were woven into it even though the fabric weave began with the blue thread. Finally, the fence around the courtyard employed the lowest grade of all. Like the other coverings over the top of the tabernacle, it employed a mere *oreg* kind of workmanship, meaning a one-color fabric with no design woven into it. As gradation is observed in the articles of furniture, so also in the fabrics.

In fact, this same principle is found in the placement of metals. Gold, the richest metal, came closest to God; silver was located at the base of the boards and copper or brass at the base of the five pillars at the door and in the courtyard.

Thus, the principle of holiness is obvious. The closer one moves toward God, the richer and holier is the construction of the tabernacle. The further one moves away from God, the cheaper and less holy is the construction. God is holy and separated from sin. Each level of gradation away from God's holiness indicates one step away from holiness and toward sin until one finds the people themselves outside of the court area living in actual attitudes and acts of sin. Perhaps, the children of Israel never fully caught sight of the theological principle expressed in all of this; namely, that on one hand God desired to dwell in their midst, but on the other hand, due to their sin, God was actually separated from them.

This conflict between God's desire to be near His people and at the same time is removed from them due to their sin brings us to the heart of tabernacle theology. The tabernacle displays forthrightly the need for reconciliation between humankind and God. The paradox between God's nearness and God's removal from sinful humankind presents a conflict that is only resolved through a sacrifice that removes the sin barrier. That sacrifice reaches its richest and fullest expression in Jesus Christ at Calvary.

Christ Brings God Near

In Jesus Christ the otherness of God has been revealed. At the same time, in Him the God who is far away is brought near. The incarnation of Christ expresses this principle beautifully. John expresses the meaning of Christ's entrance into the world in tabernacle language:

> And the Word became flesh and dwelt among us, full of grace and truth; we have beheld his glory, glory as of the only Son from the Father. John 1:14.

Here John essentially declares that God, who tabernacled among His people of old, has now tabernacled in their midst in Jesus Christ. By who Christ was, what He said, and what He did one finds the fullness of divine revelation in human form. Here the wholly other became the Word made flesh and dwelt *(skana)* in the midst of humankind![2] In Christ the glory of God—like God's glory at the tabernacle—appeared.

John says that in beholding Christ he saw God's glory. He also said in Christ he perceived grace and truth. With the ark of the covenant imagery in mind, John identifies God's grace in Christ as the fulfillment of the mercy seat. He also identifies God's truth in Christ bringing to fulfillment the law as it had been placed inside the ark!

In Christ, God Himself, who once was separated from sinful humanity in the most holy place, has come toward sinful humanity to bring about reconciliation.

The miracle of God is His love expressed in reaching out toward sinful man in His grace.

> But God shows his love for us in that while we were yet sinners Christ died for us. Romans 5:8.

> . . . in Christ God was reconciling the world to himself. . . . 2 Corinthians 5:19.

Christ the Eternal Priest

It is the intent of the New Testament to clearly depict the why, how, and fact of the formation of a new covenant between God and His people. Covenant relationship brings one to the heart of religion. Christianity is not concerned primarily with intellectual concepts, nor is it primarily concerned with ethics, but rather with one's relationship to God. It is out of the context of covenant relationship that the ethics and theology of Christianity emerge.

One of the richest interpretations of the formation of that new covenant in Jesus Christ is found in the Book of Hebrews. Here one discovers a long-sustained argument explaining carefully the steps in the formation of that new covenant relationship. The argument of the book can be summarized in one sentence. *The quality of the man determines the quality of the priestly office and the quality of the priestly office, plus the quality of the sacrifice, determines the quality of the new covenant.*

The one who mediates the covenant and the sacrifice determines its validity. The function of a priest was both to fully represent humankind and its concerns before God and to carry out the ritual of sacrifice without defilement. Consequently, the author of Hebrews begins his great argument by focusing attention upon the humanity of Jesus. In doing so he identifies the fact that Christ is able to fully understand humankind.

> For we have not a high priest who is unable to sympathize with our weaknesses, but one who in every respect has been tempted as we are, yet without sinning. Let us then with confidence draw near to the throne of grace, that we may receive mercy and find grace to help in time of need. Hebrews 4:15, 16.

Precisely in His humanity Christ achieved the highest

honor of the priestly office. As man, He suffered the pains of temptation as no other human being has suffered. Not only did he struggle with temptation in the beginning of His earthly ministry (Matthew 4:1-11), but that struggle with the forces of evil continued throughout His earthly life. However, at no point did He give in to Satan.

Here is precisely the distinguishing mark between Christ and other human priests. Whereas other human priests sinned, Jesus Christ did not sin. He was *able not to sin. Only the person who has never sinned knows the depths of temptation.* One who gives in to temptation never knows how difficult temptation can become, for he has already given in to sin. But Christ did not yield! Therefore, he knows the struggle of temptation at its deepest level!

Consequently, He is fully qualified to take up the priestly office because He knows the depths of our struggles more than any other human being! He can represent us before God better than any other priest. He is full of sympathy (Hebrews 2:14-18), is appointed by God (Hebrews 5:1, 5), and He has experienced personal preparation for the priestly office by struggling in temptation. Because of His victory over sin, Christ does not need to offer a sacrifice for His own sins (Hebrews 5:3, 8, 9).

Christ's priesthood has eternal dimensions. Unlike other priests who lived and died, thereby effecting a continual change in the priesthood from one generation to the next, Christ as the eternal Son of God is priest forever. The Book of Hebrews establishes that idea in chapter 7 where Christ's priestly order is likened to that of Melchizadek. Here the author of Hebrews exploits the silence of Genesis 14:17-20 regarding genealogy to demonstrate that there exists an eternal order of priesthood which preceded the Old Testament priestly order. This eternal order of priesthood received honor from Abraham, the father of the Hebrew people, who paid tithes to Melchizadek. In one bold stroke of the pen the author of Hebrews 7 demonstrates that Christ's priesthood, by its eternal order, surpasses the law, the sacrifices, and the old covenant. Why? Because the law, the sacrifices, and the old covenant were mediated by Moses and Aaron who were mere descendants of Abraham. Abraham himself honored the higher order of Melchizadek's priesthood.

Putting it all together, in Jesus Christ we have a Priest who is more human than other humans, yet who is eternal both in the quality and quantity of His priestly function. Thus, the author of Hebrews concludes,

> The former priests were many in number, because they were prevented by death from continuing in office; but he holds his priesthood permanently, because he continues forever. Consequently, he is able for all time to save those who draw near to God through him, since he always lives to make intercession for them. Hebrews 7:23-25.

Adding to this superior quality of priestly office, the writer quickly informs his readers that Christ serves in the heavenly sanctuary of which the Old Testament tabernacle was but a type (Hebrews 8:5).[3] These aspects fully qualify Christ to mediate a new covenant in fulfillment of the covenant promise of Jeremiah (Jeremiah 31:31-34). That new covenant is now in effect as a result of Christ's priestly and atoning work (Hebrews 8:8-13).

Ultimate Sacrifice

In Hebrews 9 Christ's sacrificial work is described. Here both the concepts of sacrifice for sin on the Day of Atonement (Leviticus 16) and the sacrifice ratifying the old covenant

(Exodus 19—24) are in mind. Hebrews 9 describes how this new sacrifice for sin is both *eternal* in its extent and *internal* in its effect. Practically speaking the one laying hold of Christ in faith experiences eternal redemption and purifying of his conscience. Neither of these took place under the old covenant.

Other New Testament writers speak of the sacrifice of Christ with the Passover setting in mind. They talk about Christ's blood through the imagery of placing the blood of a lamb on the doorposts to the dwellings of the Israelite children in Egypt. The concept of Christ as the redeeming Lamb, as One who was meek and lowly, Peter describes in these words,

> You know that you were ransomed from the futile ways inherited from your fathers, not with perishable things such as silver or gold, but with the precious blood of Christ, like that of a lamb without blemish or spot. He was destined before the foundation of the world but was made manifest at the end of the times for your sake. 1 Peter 1:18-20.

This concept of lamb reaches a beautiful climax in the Book of Revelation where the Lamb conquers the forces of evil. Rather than conquering His enemies by gun, missle, or bomb, God conquers by a meek Lamb who gives Himself to the sinful enemy in atoning sacrifice! We, too, are called to follow the teachings of Christ and the life of Christ. In our discipleship we take the way of the Lamb amidst a militaristic society.

Thus, the burden of the New Testament writers is to show that the death and resurrection of Christ rests solidly upon the concept of redemption from Egypt, the formation of the old covenant at Mt. Sinai, and all of the sacrifices pertaining to the tabernacle.

As a matter of fact, many of the steps in the Old Testament ritual of sacrifice are found in the sacrifice of Christ.

First, He is selected by God for sacrifice. Peter says He was destined for this work before the foundation of the world (1 Peter 1:20).

Second, upon Him was placed the burden of the sins of the human race. Just as the ritual of sacrifice required that the individual confess his sin over the head of the animal, thereby transferring the sin to that animal before its death, so Christ became man's sin bearer.

> All we like sheep have gone astray; we have turned every one to his own way; and the Lord has laid on him the iniquity of us all. Isaiah 53:6.

This concept of transferring sin to the sacrifice is definitely in mind in this passage from Isaiah. In the New Testament this concept achieves further clarification when Paul declares that Christ is the sin offering (2 Corinthians 5:21). This does not mean Christ became a sinner. It means He became the sin bearer or sacrifice for sin in His atoning death on the cross.

> He himself bore our sins in his body on the tree, that we might die to sin and live to righteousness. By his wounds you have been healed. 1 Peter 2:24.

Third, Christ died at Golgotha. Here the death effect of sin is clearly set forth in similar fashion to the animal dying in sacrifice at the brazen altar in the tabernacle courtyard. Before leaving the upper room, Jesus sat down with His disciples for the Passover meal.

> And as they were eating, He took bread, and blessed, and broke it, and gave it to them, and said, "Take; this is my body." And

> he took a cup, and when he had given thanks, he gave it to them, and they all drank of it. And he said to them, "This is my blood of the covenant, which is poured out for many." Mark 14:22-24.

The death of Jesus cannot be taken lightly, for it marked the point in history when God accomplished a stunning victory over the forces of evil and completed His great plan of redemption for humankind (Colossians 2:15; Ephesians 1:3-10). It affected the rending of the veil *(paroketh)* of Herod's temple known as the second temple (Mark 15:38; Matthew 27:51).

Fourth a special use of the blood took place. Christ's blood in sacrifice, symbolizing that His whole life was poured out for man's redemption, was taken into the heavenly sanctuary which the ancient tabernacle typified. As noted earlier in the description of the Old Testament sacrifices, there were two distinct acts in sacrifice. One was the death of the animal showing the effect of sin. The other was the special use of the blood in giving that animal's life up to God in sacrifice for sin to make atonement (Leviticus 17:11). Likewise, the sacrifice of Christ, described in the language of the ritual on the day of atonement, indicates He is our sin bearer, and the special use of the blood of Jesus indicates His life is given up to God for us. Thus, Paul declares,

> Who [Jesus] was put to death for our trespasses and raised for our justification. Romans 4:25.

Both the death and the resurrection of Christ stand together in the sacrifice of Christ in inaugurating the new covenant. As a result of those great acts, the benefits of this new covenant are now offered to us (Hebrews 9:15 ff.).

In addition, the sacrifice of Christ makes possible reconciliation between God and humanity. There is more than forgiveness and justification. Paul describes the atoning death of Christ in the language of the mercy seat in Romans 3:25.[4] The mercy seat at the ark of the covenant marked the spot where on the day of atonement the high priest, representing the sinful people of Israel, met face-to-face with the Holy God. Precisely of this spot God said, "There I will meet with you" (Exodus 25:22).

However, only by way of sacrifice did any meeting occur.

Now through Christ a new meeting place arises. Through the cross and resurrection of Christ it is possible for you and I to meet God and be reconciled to Him. In Christ man is both forgiven and reconciled to God.

Reconciliation brings one to the heart of the new covenant. Under the old covenant and the tabernacle three great themes arise.

- the dwelling of God;
- the holiness of God and sinfulness of man indicating alienation and separation between man and God;
- the concept of sacrifice for sin.

In Christ Jesus our Lord, these three themes finally reach their climax. Through the sacrifice of Christ, sin is removed, man is reconciled to God, and God's presence comes into the life of the Christian believer! In Him, therefore, a new covenant relationship becomes reality. It can be compared with the old covenant as follows:

Old Covenant	**New Covenant**
1. Human priest	1. Eternal priest
2. Animal sacrifice	2. Sacrifice of the Son of God
3. External forgiveness	3. Internal forgiveness
4. Reconciliation sought	4. Reconciliation completed

5. Yearly remembrance of sin	5. Eternal redemption
6. God's presence at the ark	6. God's presence in the new believer

To summarize, the quality of the new sacrifice is far greater than the old, the place of the new sacrifice supersedes the old tabernacle, and the effect of that new sacrifice supersedes the old sacrifices—all because of one Person, Jesus Christ! He, being the sinless man, made possible a better priestly office and function. His was the supreme sacrifice which made further sacrifices unnecessary. As the supreme Priest and sacrifice, He made possible a new covenant relationship between man and God that far surpasses what the people of God had experienced under the old covenant and tabernacle. The cross and resurrection of Christ, therefore, are the means of reconciliation between God and man. They effect the formation of a new covenant agreement between man and God with the promise and participation in eternal life. Christians have every right to the blessings of this new covenant. Sinners are invited to receive its benefits in exchange for alienation and loneliness by simply repenting of their sin and laying hold of Christ in faith. Those who make that commitment now experience living in the presence of God!

New Imagery

The New Testament describes this reconciled relationship between God and man through Jesus Christ in the imagery of the Old Testament.

First is the image of the Lamb. In the Old Testament the concept of the lamb arises at the Passover in Egypt (Exodus 12:1-13). In the prophet Isaiah the sacrificial lamb is identified with a person in these words:

> He was oppressed, and he was afflicted,
> yet he opened not his mouth;
> like a lamb that is led to the slaughter,
> and like a sheep that before its shearers is dumb,
> so he opened not his mouth. Isaiah 53:7.

In the intertestamental period the lamb concept is developed even further. Here the lamb takes on horns as a symbol of rulership.[5]

The New Testament picks up all of these ideas regarding the lamb and applies them to Christ. The suffering servant lamb of Isaiah 53 is united with the paschal lamb of Exodus 12 in the following passages:

> Behold, the Lamb of God, who takes away the sin of the world! John 1:29.

> . . . For Christ, our paschal lamb, has been sacrificed. 1 Corinthians 5:7.

> You know that you were ransomed from the futile ways inherited from your fathers, not with perishable things such as silver or gold, but with the precious blood of Christ, like that of a lamb without blemish or spot. 1 Peter 1:18, 19.

In the Book of Revelation the horned lamb of the intertestamental literature and the meek sacrificial Lamb are brought together.

> And between the throne and the four living creatures and among the elders, I saw a Lamb standing, as though it had been slain, with seven horns and with seven eyes. Revelation 5:6.
> "Worthy is the Lamb who was slain, to receive power and wealth and wisdom and might and honor and glory and blessing!"

> And I heard every creature in heaven and on earth and under the earth and in the sea, and all therein, saying,
> "To him who sits upon the throne and to the Lamb be blessing and honor and glory and might for ever and ever!" Revelation 5:12, 13.

The horned lamb is the slain Lamb! He rules not by guns, politics, missiles or armies, but by giving His life for the world as the sacrificial Lamb of God! Victory over all the forces of evil comes through sacrifice at the cross. The sacrificial lamb of Exodus 12 finds its fulfillment in Jesus Christ the Lamb of God who rules and reigns through that sacrificial act. The Lamb is King and rules like Yahweh ruled the people at Sinai.

Second, is the imagery of Jerusalem. In contrast to the Old Testament idea of the physical city of Jerusalem in ancient Palestine, the New Testament indicates the people of God enter the new Jerusalem as a heavenly city coming down to earth (Hebrews 12:22). John writes,

> Then I saw a new heaven and a new earth; for the first heaven and the first earth had passed away, and the sea was no more. And I saw the holy city, new Jerusalem, coming down out of heaven from God, prepared as a bride adorned for her husband; and I heard a loud voice from the throne saying, "Behold, the dwelling [tabernacle] of God is with men. He will dwell with them, and they shall be his people, and God himself will be with them. Revelation 21:1-3.

Third, is the imagery of the tabernacle and temple. In contrast to the Old Testament concept of a structure of wood and metals, the new temple is constituted by the indwelling presence of the Holy Spirit in the believer's body (1 Corinthians 6:19), in the congregation (1 Corinthians 3:16, 17), and in the whole church (Ephesians 2:21).

Thus the physical objects of the Old Testament related to Israel's spiritual life now take on fulfillment in Christ and the church.

Christ is the Reconciler. He is the Priest and sacrifice. He is the Lamb who takes away the sins of the world. Those who come to Him enter into covenant relationship with God, form the new temple, and look forward to the new Jerusalem.

My faith looks up to Thee,
  Thou Lamb of Calvary, Savior divine:
Now hear me while I pray,
  Take all my guilt away,
  O let me from this day
    Be wholly Thine.

—Ray Palmer

9
A NEW COVENANT COMMUNITY

> But you are a chosen race, a royal priesthood, a holy nation, God's own people, that you may declare the wonderful deeds of him who called you out of darkness into his marvelous light. Once you were no people but now you are God's people; once you had not received mercy but now you have received mercy. 1 Peter 2:9, 10.

With these words, Peter identified the Christian church as the new covenant community. These words obviously reflect the language of Exodus 19:6, a setting in which God formed a covenant relationship with the children of Israel after coming out of Egypt. Not only is there a new sacrifice, a new covenant, but there is also a new community of faith living in fellowship with God and with one another.

A Redeemed People

This new community is made up of persons who are redeemed in Jesus Christ. It is the community of faith. Like Israel experienced redemption from Egypt by God's great act of deliverance, so the new people of God are delivered from sin. Jesus Christ is the foundation upon which this new community rests. We are a people redeemed from sin by Jesus Christ.

To be redeemed means no less than to repent of one's sinfulness and to lay hold of God's provision in Jesus Christ. This act of faith in confessing Jesus as Lord, however, cannot be achieved merely by biological descent. Rather it calls for a voluntary decision on the part of each individual. This new redeemed people is a voluntary community of faith where each individual freely accepts God's saving work in Christ and lives under the lordship of Christ. Such a great step of faith—believing in Christ—is not an infant's activity, it is adult decision.

In contrast to the biological character of the children of Israel in the Old Testament, the new people of God arise where persons actually take the step of faith by making a responsible decision to commit themselves to Christ on a voluntary basis. No one can be forced into the people of God by infant baptism. The New Testament calls for a mature voluntary response of faith in Jesus Christ.

These redeemed people, the church, are ordinary human beings who experience God's transformation in Christ. Thus, the church is both human and divine: human in that literal human beings are converted to Christ and form this new body of people; divine in that conversion to Christ results in new spiritual life by the Holy Spirit's presence within one's life. Bender says,

> Members of the church cannot be born into the church biologically; they must choose to enter it. . . . The church is God's divine creation indeed, but it cannot exist without the human response of faith.[1]

Thus, the new people of God is a visible people. It comprises beings like you and me. It is a visible people who have been changed by God's grace in redemption. The church is not an invisible body floating around in the heavens undetectable to microscope or telescope. Rather, it is fully human persons redeemed in Christ. Just like the children of Israel were human beings living in time and space, so the new people of God are redeemed persons in Christ Jesus who live in the here and now of time and space. This new people is the visible, voluntary, redeemed people of God.

An Enlarged Community

This new covenant community is characterized by the term *ekklesia* or church. The term *ekklesia* means the called out ones. The Septuagint translation of the Hebrew Bible uses this word to translate the term *qahal*, the people of God under the old covenant. When the children of Israel encamped around the tabernacle they formed the *qahal*, the people of God under the old covenant. Now in Jesus Christ, this new community of faith is likewise known as the people living under the new covenant.

Its newness lies in the fact that the people of God are redeemed in Christ and live under His lordship. Whereas under the old covenant the people of God came from the biological descendants of Abraham, and not even all of them, now the people of God consist of all who confess Jesus is Lord. This newness applies to the quality of life in Christ Jesus and the quantity of those eligible to join the community. Now both Jew and Gentile form the new people of God. It is a multiracial, multinational, and multicultural people.

The old barriers separating people by race, nation, and culture are destroyed in Christ Jesus. At the cross hatred is removed (Ephesians 2:13-18) and those who were once no people become the people of God (Hosea 2:23; 1 Peter 2:10).

Consequently, the new people of God cannot be identified with any one nation, race, or culture. Christianity is neither a civil religion nor a cultural religion. It is not merely a renewal of Jewish tribal religion. Rather, the essence of Christianity is the gospel, the good news that all who come to Jesus Christ in repentance and faith can enter the new covenant community where no separation exists between Jew or Greek, bond or free, male or female (Galations 3:28).

This larger community not only applies to the quantity of persons who become part of the visible church, but also to the quality of life these new people live. Reconciliation in Christ means one has brought his hostility toward God to an end through repentance and entered into peace relationship with God in Christ (Romans 5:10, 11). But it also means one enters into a reconciled community with others in Christ.

> But now in Christ Jesus you who once were far off have been brought near in the blood of Christ. For he is our peace, who has made us both one, and has broken down the dividing wall of hostility, by abolishing in his flesh the law of commandments and ordinances, that he might create in himself one new man in place of the two, so making peace, and might reconcile us both to God in one body through the cross, thereby bringing the hostility to an end. Ephesians 2:13-16.

This new community of faith expresses itself in reconciled relationships between people. It is a community of *shalom*. Far too often, however, this new community perceives its life only in terms of forgiveness and justification before God and does not pursue nor discover the concept of reconciliation with God and with others in Christ. As God called Israel to live in harmony with each other as a covenant community, so church members are to live in *shalom* with each other. Amos the prophet clearly spoke about this to Israel and Judah in regard to justice and treating each other as fellow covenant community members. Today, the same concept needs application in regard to the sins of war, greed, injustice, and racial hatred.

In this new, larger, reconciled community of faith there exists a covenant bond with each other in Christ. Instead of coming to Christ as an individual and becoming part of an invisible church of disembodied spirits, one actually comes to Christ *and* to the visible body of believers. To be a Christian is not to be an isolated monk alone by oneself. Commitment to Christ also implies commitment to fellow believers in Christ, the visible body of Christ.[2] In this covenant community discipline takes place. Here people disciple each other in the obedience of Christ. Instead of the law and the ten commandments, the rule of Christ and the Sermon on the Mount become the means of discipling one another, not as a legalistic lifestyle, but as a living community of faith graced by God's Spirit to walk in this new life in Christ Jesus.

A Holy Community

This new community of faith, made up of those who have been set apart from sin, consecrates itself to the obedience and service of Christ. Christians are people indwelt by the Holy Spirit; saints of God. Peter says,

> As obedient children, do not be conformed to the passions of your former ignorance, but as he who called you is holy, be holy yourselves in all your conduct; since it is written, "You shall be holy, for I am holy." 1 Peter 1:14-16.

The idea of a holy community is so important that the New Testament calls it the temple of God (1 Corinthians 3:16, 17; 6:19; Ephesians 2:19-22). The imagery in mind for this designation is none other than the Old Testament tabernacle with its most holy place. The Greek term for temple used in these passages is *naos,* a term applied to the temple at Jerusalem during the kingdom period and Herod's temple. However, the place where the ark of the covenant rested, prior to the building of the temple of Solomon (1 Samuel 3:3), is called the *naos* in the Septuagint translation. From this we learn that the New Testament idea of the church is the very holy dwelling place of God. Two great themes from the Old Testament, the dwelling place of God and the people of God, converge in the church as God's new people. Christians are as holy as the most holy place of that ancient tabernacle!

Once redeemed by Christ, Christians no longer live far removed from the divine presence. They are brought directly into God's holy presence. God dwells *(mishkan)* in them as He dwelt in the most holy place of the Old Testament tabernacle. This truth is significant for an understanding of the new people of God in contrast to the former people of God. First, it indicates that the desire to reconcile sinful man with God in the Old Testament tabernacle through animal sacrifices has been completed in Jesus Christ. Those far off are now brought directly into God's presence through Christ. In fact, all Christians today can live closer to God than the high priest in the Old Testament!

Second, this concept implies that the new community of faith must live out its ethical conduct according to its high and holy calling. The church is not on its own to determine its behavior in life. Rather it is called to live out holiness as demonstrated in Jesus Christ. It takes the commands of Christ seriously and orders its life accordingly. Christ is not only the basis for our redemption, He is also the norm of our ethical conduct.

Third, this concept implies that which the tabernacle symbolized, namely God's dwelling among the people, has now reached its fulfillment. Whereas God once dwelt *among* His people, today He dwells *in* them. The church becomes the dwelling place of God through the Spirit (Ephesians 2:22). In life and conduct the new people of God demonstrate in the world what it means to be God's holy temple as the Spirit of God permeates its life.

A Kingdom People

> Now after John was arrested, Jesus came into Galilee, preaching the gospel of God, and saying, "The time is fulfilled, and the kingdom of God is at hand; repent, and believe in the gospel." Mark 1:14, 15.

The main theme of Jesus' teaching was the kingdom of God. People are invited to enter into this new kingdom by way of the new birth. Through repentance Christ enters into and rules in their lives.

This kingdom is the eschatological kingdom to which the Old Testament looked forward. The early church leaders identified the resurrection of Christ, His ascension, and exaltation as the entrance into His messianic reign.

At Pentecost, Peter declared:

> This Jesus God raised up, and of that we all are witnesses. Being therefore exalted at the right hand of God, and having received from the Father the promise of the Holy Spirit, he has poured out this which you see and hear. For David did not ascend into the heavens; but he himself says, "The Lord said to my lord, Sit at my right hand, till I make thy enemies a stool for thy feet." Let all the house of Israel therefore know assuredly that God has made him both Lord and Christ, this Jesus whom you crucified. Acts 2:32-36.

Stephen said that God does not dwell in houses made with hands, referring to the tabernacle. Rather heaven is His throne and the earth is His footstool (Acts 7:47-49).

Paul said in Colossians 1:13:

> He has delivered us from the dominion of darkness and transferred us to the kingdom of his beloved Son.

To these passages one could add all of the New Testament quotes and allusions to Psalm 110:1 in which the messianic reign of Christ is identified.

Perhaps this great truth finds greater expression in the early church's basic confession of faith, namely, "Jesus is Lord."[3] In this confession the name for Yahweh Himself was conferred upon Christ. To be a Christian one confesses that there are no other lords, but one, namely Jesus Christ. To say Jesus is Lord meant no earthly Roman Caesar could receive ultimate allegiance by the early church. By refusing to say Caesar is Lord, these early Christians suffered martyrdom, yet they steadfastly refused to misuse the term "Lord."

Paul carefully describes this highly exalted position of Christ.[4] For him Christ is *now* reigning in His messianic kingdom. However, while the New Testament clearly affirms the kingship of the Lord Jesus Christ, it also identifies both a present reality of the kingdom and a future dimension to it.

The people of God form an eschatological people who participate in the final kingdom. That participation is already taking place. Yet the new people of God still live in the midst of an evil age. Perhaps this is best explained by the fact that two ages overlap, this age and the age to come. The new people of God have already entered into that new age to come and thereby participate in the kingdom now. But the fullness of that kingdom has not yet fully arrived. Therefore, the kingdom is now, but not yet.[5]

All of this affirms the view that the church, as people under the rule of Christ, forms this new community of faith in which Jesus is Lord. Under the old covenant in its earliest life the people of Israel lived in the encampment around the tabernacle with God ruling over them. The term which describes that form of kingship is *theocracy,* the rule of God over His people. When they rejected God and turned to human kings like the other nations, God expressed disappointment (1 Samuel 8:4 ff). Changing from God as king to a human monarchy, and later to the divided kingdoms of Israel and Judah with human political kings, became a major move away from their earlier life under the theocracy. The prophets again and again called Israel's attention to the earlier model of the covenant and the theocracy even through the period of the monarchy and the divided kingdoms.

The early church found its model in Israel's early life, the theocratic period. For them the key to understanding the kingdom of God and the new people of God was the theocracy with God ruling over them rather than human political kings. Thus, the New Testament concept of the Kingdom of God knows no geographical, racial, or cultural boundaries. Rather, where Jesus is Lord, there the kingdom is present.

This reign of Christ expresses itself in His lordship over the church as the new people of God. This new covenant community living under His lordship is the highest and grandest possession God has on this earth (Ephesians 1). Nothing shall surpass it in this world. When this rule of Christ reaches its grand purpose and end *(telos),* He will deliver the kingdom to the Father that God may be all in all (1 Corinthians 15:28). The following diagram expresses this kingdom concept:

Old Covenant	**New Covenant**
Theocracy	Christocracy
(Rule of God)	(Rule of Christ)
People Under This Rule	**People Under This Rule**
(qahal)	*(ekklesia)*
tabernacle encampment	Church

Jeremiah's promise of a new covenant now finds fulfillment in the church. A new covenant came into being through a new sacrifice. A new knowledge of God exists on the basis of an experiential relationship with Christ. A new kind of fellowship within the covenant community finds expression in the bonds of brotherhood and covenant relationship. A new kind of forgiveness in Christ Jesus, both internal and eternal, is now available. In this new covenant community the church becomes both God's dwelling place and God's people.

> So then you are no longer strangers and sojourners, but you are fellow citizens with the saints and members of the household of God, built upon the foundation of the apostles and prophets, Christ Jesus himself being the cornerstone, in whom the whole structure is joined together and grows into a holy temple in the Lord; in whom you also are built into it for a dwelling place of God in the Spirit. Ephesians 2:19-22.

Occasionally persons ask why Christians express interest in the tabernacle. Why build a reproduction of it for tourists to see? I answer by stating that one cannot fully comprehend nor appreciate Christ and His church without knowing this Old Testament background. When tourists ask what the tabernacle has to do with Mennonites, I answer it has no more to do with Mennonites than any other Christian group.

It does, however, carry a tremendous amount of background meaning to an understanding of the New Testament church. And it is to that model of the church in the New Testament to which Mennonites and other Christian groups want to be true.

> I love Thy kingdom, Lord,
>   The house of Thine abode,
> The church our blest Redeemer saved
>   With His own precious blood.
> I love Thy church, O God,
>   Her walls before Thee stand,
> Dear as the apple of Thine eye,
>   And graven on Thy hand.
>
> —Timothy Dwight

10
HEAVENLY TABERNACLE

In the previous pages an attempt has been made to unfold the meaning and construction of the tabernacle. Obviously, some matters of construction and interpretation are debatable and you may not agree with everything I have said. I have tried to elucidate the central ideas and from these move out toward the details.

Obviously, my view centers in the concept of God's dwelling as the heart of the tabernacle. I have traced that dwelling from the tabernacle to Christ and to the Christian church. God's divine presence with His people finds its grand climax in the heavenly scene. Note the following verse from the Apostle John who heard the voice of God from the throne of heaven saying:

> Behold, the dwelling *(skana, mishkan)* of God is with men. He will dwell with them, and they shall be his people, and God himself will be with them; he will wipe away every tear from their eyes, and death shall be no more, neither shall there be mourning nor crying nor pain any more, for the former things have passed away. Revelation 21:3, 4.

This verse leads one to a major concept regarding the tabernacle, namely, that it reaches its grand climax in the heavenly setting. In this heavenly dwelling man is no longer tempted to sin. God and His people dwell together in sweet harmony throughout eternity. It is the ultimate in covenant relationship between God and His people. They dwell in God's presence and God tabernacles with them in the fullest sense of the word.

This future view of God's dwelling with His people gives us the key by which to interpret the central Bible teaching regarding God's dwelling. Twice in the Old Testament and twice in the New Testament we read of God's command to Moses to build the tabernacle "according to the pattern which was shown Moses on the mountain" (Exodus 25:40; Numbers 8:4; Acts 7:44; Hebrews 8:5). We cannot be sure what Moses saw on the mountain. Many interpret these words to mean all the physical details of the tabernacle were shown to Moses by God. Others reject that idea entirely since it reflects a Platonic philosophy.

May I venture a different guess? Could it be possible that Moses got a glimpse into the apocalyptic heavenly scene from which he discovered by divine revelation the grand beauty of God's dwelling with His people where there is no more sin and temptation? If my idea is correct, then the ancient tabernacle was patterned after the concept of God's dwelling with His redeemed people. Not only does this give us a hint into what Moses saw, it also provides a major step in understanding the concept of types in the tabernacle. God's ultimate, heavenly dwelling with His people is the grand climax of all that has been typified. According to one writer,

> This apocalyptic view of the dwelling of God with man is the summum bonum of typology.[1]

Moses took that concept of God's dwelling and built a

tabernacle after it thereby giving Israel a little glimpse into the grand climax of God's working in history. Due to their sin, the fullness of God's dwelling was not experienced by them, but it was there in typological form pointing forward in history.

When they dedicated the first temple, God's presence came upon the scene. Although Israel tended to confine God to the temple over against His mobility with the tabernacle, the concept of God's dwelling with them remained alive.

We reach another step in the progression when Jesus came into the world:

> And the Word became flesh and dwelt *(skana, mishkan)* among us, full of grace and truth; we have beheld his glory, glory as of the only Son from the Father. John 1:14.

Presently, God dwells in His people, His redeemed body, the church. And wherever God's people are found throughout the world today, there God Himself dwells.

Finally and ultimately a grand finale awaits us when God dwells in and with His people forever. Heaven will be a grand experience in which we all will tabernacle with God eternally. Its glory and beauty may not be so much the physical features of streets and buildings as much as the joy of being in His presence. With Christ the Lamb of God visibly before us, and no more storms and stresses in life, we all will sing the blessed chorus to God and to Christ. It is then and only then that the typology of the ancient tabernacle will have reached its complete fulfillment.

I have a feeling that some interpreters stress so much the *quantity* of Old Testament types that they miss their *quality.* Again and again persons visiting the tabernacle want to tell me about the little types I missed in my presentation. Yet when I consider these interpretations how often they reveal a shortsighted understanding of the tabernacle. How I wish my friends would worry less about the types of Christ in the color scheme, for example, and catch the vision of God's dwelling with His people *now* and in the heavenly scene.

Thus, in these pages we have looked at the ancient tabernacle with its intricate details, but far more important, we have moved from promise to fulfillment, from the Old Testament to God's fuller Word in the New Testament. God's dwelling in embryonic form in the Old Testament tabernacle now reaches its beautiful fulfillment in Christ and the new covenant people, the church.

We await the final step, the heavenly tabernacle, where we will discover how little we know now about God's dwelling among His people. After we share in that heavenly dwelling we will begin to realize how important was our coming to Jesus Christ who is the way for going, the truth for knowing, and the life for living. Without Him, after all, we wouldn't get there.

APPENDIX I

The Problem of Interpretation

In lecturing to tourists on the tabernacle, various interpretations have come to my attention. Perhaps no more than 10 percent of the Jewish folks who go through the tabernacle express dismay at the Christological interpretation of its types. Mormons tell me, "We *have* a temple, too," to which I reply, "We *are* the temple of God." Masons are quick to point out that "Jesus was a Mason" to which I reply, "Where do you read that in the New Testament?"

I have also met persons who were disturbed because I did not interpret all the detailed parts of the tabernacle as types of Christ. So the problem of interpretation requires serious study. Most persons, however, have expressed appreciation for my interpretation.

Origin of the Tabernacle

A major concern is the origin of the tabernacle. Did the tabernacle and its accompanying sacrifices arise in a vacuum by direct command of God with no outside religious influence? Or, was there some borrowing from other Near Eastern religions?

On the one hand there are some who say the tabernacle and Israel's worship life, including the sacrifices, were merely borrowed from her neighbors. On the other hand, there are those who say none of it was borrowed, that it came in its entirety from God.

Roland de Vaux, in his extensive studies, has clearly shown that some of the concepts expressed in the tabernacle are also found in

Mesopotamia, Syria, and Phoenicia.[1] But although there is similarity of ideas and practices, the differences are even more pronounced. Israel did not borrow indiscriminately. Its religion was not a hodgepodge of other pagan ideas. If Israel borrowed from other Near Eastern religions, it borrowed *only* that which was compatible with its belief in Yahweh.[2] And when it borrowed other religious practices *their meaning was changed* so that, in actual practice, it conformed to the commands of God. As H. H. Rowley says:

> Israel took over very much, whose *origin* is therefore to be sought further back. Its *meaning*, however, is not necessarily to be sought further back. Often it was readopted and made the vehicle of her own faith and her own thought, and we have no right to assume that it was taken over unaltered in form or meaning. For there was an element in her religion which she did not derive from any other people, but which was mediated to her through her own religious leaders, and especially Moses, and what she took over was integrated into her own religion and made to serve its ends.[3]

It seems more appropriate to say that the tabernacle originated by command of God in the midst of the world in which Israel found herself. These commands resulted in a physical structure that has some similarities with other Near Eastern temples, but the meaning and use of these structures were far removed from the polytheistic worship activities of the Canaanites, Syrians, Phoenicians and Mesopotamians. Just as Israel saw the pagan Egyptian gods crumble, so it saw the polytheistic gods of other Near Eastern religions crumble. Only Yahweh was to be served. And the tabernacle was built at His command and used to worship only Him.

Determining the Text

A second major problem of interpretation is the texts which describe the tabernacle. Recent studies on the tabernacle narratives have proliferated as a result of new understandings of the literary development of the Pentateuch and the tie between Israel's worship and history.[4]

For some time Old Testament scholars have set forth the view, based on a literary analysis, that the first five books of the Old Testament come from four separate documents (J-E-D-P) written at different times during Israel's history. The late liberal scholar Wellhausen proposed the theory that the tabernacle narratives were written by the priests after the Exile. He said the priests "created" the tabernacle at this late date and projected it backward into Israel's history in order to substantiate the concept of monotheism. Therefore, the tabernacle was a pious fraud according to Wellhausen.

But today Wellhausen's theory is soundly rejected. Even those today who hold to the documentary view of the Pentateuch believe that the tabernacle was in existence long before the temple. According to the documentary view, the tabernacle is referred to in the earliest documents (J and E). Some think there are two ancient literary sources which talk about two shrine traditions in ancient Israel; one dealing with the ark of the covenant in the E document and the other dealing with the tent of meeting in the J document.[5] According to this view, these sacred objects remained separated until after the children of Israel entered the Promised Land. Thereupon the tabernacle was built at Shiloh and the ark of the covenant was placed inside its most holy place.

In the period of time leading up to this union of "tent of meeting" and ark of the covenant, after which the tent of meeting became tabernacle at Shiloh, the tent of meeting was kept in the northern part of the tribal settlement in Palestine and the ark of the covenant among the southern tribes. It was, therefore, moved from Shechem to Gilgal, then to Shiloh, and finally to Jerusalem.[6] According to this interpretation, the P document, containing much of the books of Exodus and Leviticus, was written by the priests around the time of the Exile to explain the tabernacle and sacrifices in their fullness in order to help the children of Israel theologically. Due to the Exile, the children of Israel, as Psalm 137 indicates, found it difficult to sense God's presence in Babylon and, in fact, thought God was still back in Jerusalem. The P document, therefore, sets forth the idea of the tabernacle with its theology of God as One who is not confined at one spot, but always leads His people. He is a moving, acting God, not a stationary God of sacred temples. The tabernacle, in its fullest description, became for the priests the best illustration that Yahweh had always been a moving, active God among His people even before the temple was erected.

How shall we respond to this interpretation? First, we can be grateful for the new emphasis upon the tent of meeting and ark of the covenant coming from the Sinai setting. Thanks to Frank M. Cross, Wellhausen's view of the tabernacle as a pious fraud has been completely rejected in contemporary Old Testament studies.[7] Second, even if the tabernacle narratives were written by the priests at the time of the Exile, this does not discredit the *origin* of the tabernacle at Sinai. For the time of writing of the documents has very little to do with the time when the actual events took place. As Anderson says,

> Although the priestly work (P) was finally written down only in the period after the fall of the nation in 587 BC, actually it preserves many ancient recollections. In dealing with biblical literature, it is axiomatic that the *date of writing is no sure index of the age of the traditions it records.*[8]

We must remember truth passed from one generation to the next by oral tradition, which, incidentally, is far more reliable than we may think. Therefore, the tabernacle itself existed long before it was completely described by the priests. Even if one follows the documentary view of the Pentateuch, he is led to the conclusion that Israel had a central sanctuary as the center of its worship life from its earliest beginnings at Mount Sinai.[9]

Third, while contemporary Old Testament studies show the ark of the covenant and tent of meeting as separate traditions which later combined with the completed tabernacle at Shiloh, I tend to think that the tabernacle as described in the Exodus narratives existed even in the desert. Despite the literary problems, the narrative states the actual time when the tabernacle was set up, namely, at the beginning of the second year after deliverance from Egypt (Exodus 40:17). Numbers 33 carefully describes each place of encampment in the wilderness. If the tabernacle did not exist early in Israel's history, how are we to account for these passages?

Fourth, while the tent of meeting preceded the building of the tabernacle, the theological implications of it were transferred to the tabernacle. When this actually happened is not entirely solved in my mind. Hopefully, further study will clarify this matter. The time of the beginning of the tabernacle, however, is not as important as its theological meaning for the people.

Tabernacle Vocabulary

There are several Hebrew terms used to describe the ancient tabernacle. Each contributes its own shade of meaning for our understanding of the purpose for this ancient structure.

First is *'ohel moed,* which occurs in Exodus 33:7-11; Numbers 11:16, 17, 24-30; 12; Deuteronomy 31:14-15. The term is translated "tent of meeting" and can mean the tent of the congregation where Israel gathered together or the tent of meeting where God revealed Himself and met with His people. It implied a conscious interrelationship between God and His people.[10] For example, in Exodus 33:7-11 God met Moses at the door of his tent and manifested Himself. The transcendent God *met* with Israel's highest authority. While *'ohel moed* preceded the building of the tabernacle, the idea of God meeting with His people was transferred to the tabernacle's most holy place and the ark of the covenant. In giving instructions for building the ark of the covenant, God said,

> There I will meet with you, and from above the mercy seat, from between the two cherubim that are upon the ark of the testimony, I will speak with you of all that I will give you in commandment for the people of Israel. Exodus 25:22.

In short, the concept of *'ohel moed* implied the tabernacle had something to do with the relationship between God and His people. It was a place where the two met face-to-face.

A second term used to describe the tabernacle is *'ohel* which means tent, tabernacle, or dwelling.[11] Prior to Exodus 25 it is always translated *tent,* but in the tabernacle narratives it is translated *tabernacle* in the first narrative (Exodus 25—31) and *tent* in the second narrative (Exodus 35—40).[12] Obviously, the tabernacle was a physical structure. The tent idea applied to the tabernacle since it was an accepted housing pattern among the children of Israel as far back as Abraham (Genesis 12:8; 13:3, 5). At times spiritual experiences took place at the door of one's tent as, for example, when Abraham met the Lord in the plains of Mamre (Genesis 18:1) or when Moses met the Lord at the door of his tent (Exodus 33:7-11). While the term is applied specifically to the second covering over the top of the tabernacle, its basic meaning is the physical structure sometimes translated interchangeably tabernacle and tent.

A third and closely related term is *mishkan.*[13] This word does not appear before Exodus 25:9 and where it appears in the tabernacle narratives, it is always translated *tabernacle.* It comes from the Hebrew root *shakan,* which means to dwell together as neighbors.[14] It has the idea of pitching a tent and sitting down and dwelling in a certain place. This is the major term used to describe the tabernacle. *Mishkan* takes us beyond a mere physical structure to God's abode, his presence in the midst of His people. It speaks of the imminence of God and is expressed in the command to Moses:

> And let them make me a sanctuary, that I may dwell in their midst. Exodus 25:8.

The relationship between *tent and tabernacle* can be compared to the relationship between the English terms house and home. House refers primarily to the physical structure, whereas home implies a quality of life lived by people inside that physical structure.

Mishkan means God's dwelling whereas *'ohel* speaks of the physical structure in which He dwelt. We, therefore, should not be surprised that the Septuagint translators used the same Greek work, *skana,* to translate both Hebrew terms, but it is the concept of *mishkan,* or dwelling, which is the dominant meaning when *skana* appears in the New Testament.[15] Thus, the biblical writers emphasized the concept of God's abiding presence with His people more than the physical structure in which He dwells.

Other terms used, rather infrequently, are "tent of witness," "holy place," and "sanctuary." The idea of witness came from the presence of the Ten Commandments in the ark of the covenant, thereby declaring God's solemn claims upon the people. And the term "holy place" *(miqdash)* or "sanctuary" emphasized the holiness of the tabernacle. It was a sacred place consecrated to God.

Therefore, from a linguistic point of view, the tabernacle was: (1) a physical structure, (2) a place where God dwelt or His abode in the midst of the people, (3) a structure set aside for sacred use and consecrated for divine service, and (4) it provided a setting where a holy God and a sinful people met each other. As "tent of meeting" and "dwelling," the tabernacle possessed the qualities and heart of Israel's worship life.

Interpreting Types

The interpretation of the tabernacle brings one to different conclusions and applications depending on how one interprets types. Most fundamental to the question of interpretation is typology, a study of types. Here we discover the extremes, from those who see types of Christ in every detail of the tabernacle to those who see virtually no typological significance in the tabernacle at all. The problem becomes more serious, however, when we recognize that the distance between extremism in typology and the allegorizing of Scripture is very short indeed. Allegorism is a method of interpreting the text of Scripture which regards the literal sense as a vehicle for a secondary more spiritual and profound sense. This method of interpretation arose among the pagan Greeks. It was taken up by the Alexandrian Jews through Philo and later adopted by the Christian church where it dominated biblical interpretation until the time of the Reformation. Luther called it *aufenspiel*. The problem with allegorism, as Bernard Ramm properly states, is that,

> it obscures the true meaning of the Word of God. There are no controls on the imagination of the interpreter, so the Bible becomes putty in the hands of each interpreter.[16]

For example, Clement of Alexandria found typological significance in every detail of the tabernacle:

> In the midst of the covering and veil, where the priests were allowed to enter, was situated the altar of incense, the symbol of the earth placed in the middle of the universe. . . . Now the high priest's robe is the symbol of the world of sense. The seven planets are represented by the five stones and the two carbuncles, for Saturn and the moon.[17]

This kind of extremism brought a conservative reaction, later in the church, by Bishop Marsh who developed what is known in typology as Marsh's principle: *A type is only a type if the New Testament calls it a type*.

This principle has exerted a tremendous influence upon those who study typology. Most expositors follow Marsh's principle often to its exact letter or at least the spirit of it.

Perhaps the best advice for the tabernacle interpreter in regard to types comes from Wallace B. Nicholson. He says that

> The type must have some historical basis in scripture; it must bear a *notable* resemblance to the antitype; *it must bear competent evidence that it was divinely appointed as a type;* it must be a type, susceptible of only one meaning; if typical it must not be of a sinful nature. Nothing in scripture can be considered a proper type which does not possess these characteristics. The type must be sharply distinguished from allegory and the *exposition of allegorical scripture* should not be confused with the *allegorical* exposition of scripture.[18]

Several New Testament passages clearly identify the tabernacle as typological (Hebrews 8:5; 9:9, 24; 10:1). Note these words,

> For Christ has entered, not into a sanctuary made with hands, a copy *(antitupa)* of the true one, but into heaven itself, now to appear in the presence of God on our behalf. Hebrews 9:24.

Obviously, the New Testament identified both the present and future as having some typological tie to the ancient Hebrew tabernacle. But this does not mean every detail of the tabernacle was typological. It was typological *as a whole* of something greater and only insofar as the individual parts support that whole are they typological.

Consequently, I believe there are secondary types in the tabernacle that support its major concept, but these secondary types are not to receive primary attention. Primary attention is to be focused upon the totality of the tabernacle as a type pointing forward to the incarnate and sacrificial work of Christ as a tabernacle (John 1:14), to the church as the temple of God (Ephesians 2:19-22), and to heaven as the final "tabernacling" of God with His people (Revelation 21:3). The parts and details are typological *only* insofar as they contribute to this primary typological outlook.

A type is the impression of the real. As the real is impressed upon something, it leaves its mark. The tabernacle is the impression of Christ, of the church, and of heaven. These are the reality of what was typified in the ancient tabernacle. The tabernacle, however, is more than type. It is a symbol of man's relationship with God when seen in the entirety of the sacrifices. The *real* fellowship between man and God was lost in the fall (Genesis 3). The tabernacle points in its symbolic character back toward the real fellowship man needs with His Creator. But it also points forward to the restoration of that fellowship through Jesus Christ. This is where it becomes a type pointing forward to Christ and the church. But the writer to the Hebrews indicates there is one more step in the process, namely, heaven, where the real is once more fully attained (Hebrews 9:24; Revelation 21:3). Thus, we have come full circle. In my judgment, no study of the types of the tabernacle is complete unless one has gone the full circle. We cannot stop with the tabernacle as a type of Christ. We must also ask, how does it typify the church and finally, how does it point forward to heaven?

Thus, the principles upon which I work at interpreting the tabernacle may be stated as follows:

First, an attempt is made to discover the meaning of the tabernacle as built and used in its historical setting; seeking to determine its central meaning as it pertains to God's dwelling in the midst of His people, their separation from him because of sin, his meeting with them, and how the worship of the children of Israel expressed itself through the sacrifices and articles of furniture in the ancient tabernacle.

Second, I attempt to find the New Testament resemblance, either specifically named or implied, as I move from God's dwelling in the tabernacle (Exodus 25:8), to his dwelling in Christ (John 1:14), to the Christian church as His temple (Ephesians 2:19-22), and to heaven itself (Revelation 21:3), the ultimate dwelling of God.

Third, I give attention to Old Testament worship viewed as God and man meeting together by way of sacrifice and the New Testament concept of worship based on the sacrificial death of Christ with the new covenant through which man and God meet in genuine reconciliation.

Fourth, the primary and central meaning of each part of the tabernacle is explained as it contributes to the whole. Secondary types are mentioned in an appendix.

In taking this approach all allegorism and extreme typology is rejected. I keep close to Marsh's principle, but am not limited by it. Accordingly, this book may not agree with a good number of works on the tabernacle. But, in my judgment, it will agree with what I believe is the biblical concept of the tabernacle. So be it.

APPENDIX II
Secondary Types

In contrast to the emphasis given in this book some tabernacle scholars believe all the details of the tabernacle have typological meaning. Accordingly, several types are listed below as secondary and may be seen in the tabernacle as they contribute to its central meaning.

A. Metals
   1. Gold—type of deity.
   2. Silver—type of redemption.
   3. Brass—type of judgment.

B. Colors
   1. Blue—type of the heavenly character of Christ.
   2. Purple—type of royalty of Christ.
   3. Red—type of the redemption of Christ.
   4. White—type of the righteousness of Christ.

C. Fabrics
   1. Fine linen—type of the righteousness of Christ.
   2. Goats hair—type of the serviceableness of Christ.
   3. Rams skins dyed red—type of the redemption of Christ.

D. Brazen Altar—type of the redemption of Christ.

E. Laver—type of the Word of God.

F. Oil in the lampstand—type of the Holy Spirit.

G. Wood—type of the humanity of Christ.

H. Bars—type of the unifying work of the Holy Spirit.

NOTES

Chapter 1

1. D. W. Gooding has made an exhaustive study of the tabernacle narratives both from the Masoretic Text and the Septuagint. Both narratives were translated by the same translator, Gooding suggests, and perhaps a later editor worked on Exodus 38. While there are differences in content, Gooding does not see any major differences in principle between the two texts. When differences of order appear, Gooding suggests they are due to a rearrangement of the Greek text later rather than by the original Septuagint translators or the original Hebrew text. For more on this, see D. W. Gooding, *The Account of the Tabernacle*, (Cambridge: The University Press, 1959).

2. A Jewish commentary says, "The ten plagues form a symmetrical and regularly unfolding scheme. The first nine plagues consist of three series of three each: (a) blood, frogs, gnats; (b) fleas, murrain, boils; (c) hail, locusts, darkness. In each series the first plague is announced to Pharaoh beforehand at the brink of the Nile, the second is proclaimed by Moses at the Palace, and the third is sent without warning. Each series of plagues rises to a climax, the final series is the climax of all that preceded; and these are but the prelude to the tenth plague—the death of the firstborn, which seals the completeness of the whole.... Moreover, the context was far more than a dramatic humiliation of the unrepentant and infatuated tyrant. It was nothing less than a judgment on the gods of Egypt. The plagues fell on the principal divinities that were worshipped since times immemorial in the Nile Valley. The river was a god; it became loathsome to its worshippers. The frog was venerated as the sign of fruitfulness, and it was turned into horror. The cattle—the sacred ram, the sacred goat, the sacred bull—were all smitten. The sacred bettle became a torment to those who put their trust in its divinity. When we add to these the plague of darkness, which showed the eclipse of Ra, the Sun-god, we

see that we have here a contrast between the God of Israel, the Lord of the Universe, and the senseless idols of a senile civilization; as it is written (xii, 12, 'against all the gods of Egypt I will execute judgments: I am the Lord.' ") J. R. Hertz (Editor), *The Pentateuch and Haftorahs* (2nd. Edition: London: Soncino Press, 5734—1973, Sixteenth Impression), p. 400.

3. Millard C. Lind,*Biblical Foundations for Christian Worship* (Scottdale: Herald Press, 1973), p. 26.

4. Bernhard W. Anderson, *Understanding the Old Testament*, Third Edition (Englewood Cliffs, New Jersey: Prentice-Hall, Inc., 1975), p. 93.

5. Samson Raphael Hirsch, *The Pentateuch*, Vol. II, translated by Isaac Levy (2nd Edition; New York: Bloch Publishing Company, 1960), p. 429.

6. Frank Cross says, "While the J stratum strongly emphasized the covenant at Sinai, and E describes both the revelation of Yahweh's name and the formation of the covenant in the desert, it is particularly the tabernacle traditions which maintain that Yahweh was first worshipped in the desert, and that the cultic institutions and the formation of the state (which P correctly identifies as being one: the amphictyonic system is a simple and primitive form of theocracy) find their origin under Moses in the desert." See Frank M. Cross, Jr., "The Tabernacle," *The Biblical Archeologist*, Vol. X, No. 3 (September 1947), p. 52.

7. John Bright, *The Kingdom of God* (New York, Nashville: Abingdon Press, 1953), p. 28.

8. Olford writes, "It seems quite clear from reading the Book of Exodus that it took two-and-a-half to three months to reach Mount Sinai: 'In the third month, when the children of Israel were gone forth out of the land of Egypt, the same day came they into the wilderness of Sinai' (Exodus 19:1). They remained at the foot of Sinai forty days, for we read that 'Moses was in the mount forty days and forty nights' (Exodus 24:18). That brings the time lapse to some four-and-a-half months. It appears evident that it was after Moses came down from the mount that the work of making the tabernacle began (See Exodus 34:32; 35:4, 20, 30). The date of its completion and erection was New Year's Day. 'On the first day of the [first] month in the second year, on the first day of the month . . . the tabernacle was reared up' (Exodus 40:17). Thus, if we subtract four-and-a-half months from twelve, we have seven-and-a-half, suggesting that the actual making of the tabernacle took something like seven-and-a-half to eight months." Stephen F. Olford, *The Tabernacle; Camping with God* (Neptune, New Jersey: Loizeaux Brothers, 1971), p. 52.

9. Lewis says, "This tent of meeting was set up soon after crossing the Red Sea—initiatory for the establishment of the worship of Jehovah as against Egyptian worship, erected under, or at the foot of Mt. Horeb, sanctified to this and prior to the giving of the law. It was occupied only

by Moses and Joshua until the *Tabernacle of the Testimony* was built, as directed by Jehovah, in which the forthcoming law was to be deposited." G. Wilton Lewis, *The Tabernacle of the Testimony* (Cincinnati: The Standard Publishing Company, 1925), p. 5.

10. W. G. Rhind, *The Tabernacle in the Wilderness; the Shadow of Heavenly Things,* (London: Samuel Bagster and Sons, Paternoster Row, Fourth Edition, 1845), p. 11.

11. Spink suggests a total area of twelve miles, but we cannot be sure of this estimate. See James F. Spink, *Types and Shadows of Christ in the Tabernacle,* (New York, Loizeaux Brothers, 1946), pp. 35, 36.

12. James Strong, *The Tabernacle of Israel in the Desert* (Grand Rapids: Baker Book House, 1952), p. 12.

13. For a fuller treatment of this subject, see the article "Cubit" in *The International Standard Bible Encyclopedia,* Vol. II (Grand Rapids: Wm. B. Eerdmans Publishing Company, 1939), p. 765.

14. Moshe Levine, *The Tabernacle: Its Structure and Utensils* (New York London. Jerusalem: The Soncino Press Limited, 1969), p. 74.

15. See Leviticus 3:2, 8, 13; 7:29-30; 8:3, 4; 14:11, 12, 23, 24; Numbers 5:16-25; 6:10-20; 8:9-13; 10:3; 16:19.

16. Haran says it was a mixture of dyed wool with linen according to the *roqem* workmanship. See Menahem Haran, "The Priestly Image of the Tabernacle," *Hebrew Union College Annual,* Vol. XXXVI (1965), p. 225.

Chapter 2

1. The acacia tree has a lovely fragrance. It is a genus of the *Leguminosal* or pea family containing about 450 species of plants ranging in size from small shrubs such as *Acacia Myrtifolia* to thirty-foot trees such as *Acacia Multispicata.* The term acacia is derived from a Greek word meaning "thorn" or "point" which refers to the sharp spines found in some species. The Egyptians used the wood for the coffins of the pharaohs because of its lasting qualities. *Acacia seyal* is thought to be the wood referred to in the tabernacle narratives of the Bible. Acacia wood, with its lovely fragrance, is used for furniture. The bark is used for tanning and the flowers for perfume. It can also be used for making soap, shampoo, medicine, fiber, and dye. The acacia tree cannot tolerate cold weather and, therefore, grows in warm climates such as California and Florida in the United States. It also grows in Egypt and other parts of Africa and Australia.

2. See Menehan Haran, "The Priestly Image of the Tabernacle," *Hebrew Union College Annual,* Vol. XXXVI (1965), p. 224.

3. Henry W. Soltau, *The Holy Vessels and Furniture of the Tabernacle* (Grand Rapids: Kregel Publications, Reprint of the 1851 Edition), p. 133.

4. The Ras Shamra texts show the tie between Israel's sacrifices and other pagan sacrifices. See H. H. Rowley, *Worship in Ancient Israel: Its Forms and Meaning* (Philadelphia: Fortress Press, 1967), pp. 112, 113 for a fuller explanation of this relationship.

5. Rowley's books, *From Moses to Qumran* and *Worship in Ancient Israel: Its Forms and Meaning* (Philadelphia: Fortress Press, 1967) are helpful on this question. John Bright says, "Yet Israel did not borrow indiscriminately but rather tended to take over only what was compatible with Yahwism, and to supply that with a new rationale." John Bright, *A History of Israel* (Philadelphia: The Westminster Press, 1959), p. 149.

6. H. H. Rowley, *Worship in Ancient Israel: Its Forms and Meaning* (Philadelphia: Fortress Press, 1967), p. 113.

7. H. H. Rowley, *From Moses to Qumran*, (New York: Association Press, 1963), p. 91.

8. Quoted by Rowley in *Worship in Ancient Israel: Its Forms and Meaning, op. cit.*, p. 134.

9. Hirsch says, "We believe that חטאת is formed from the Piel meaning of the root חטא , and so, need not necessarily, as a "sin offering," presume a sin committed, but as "freeing from sin" is to bring about the resolution to keep free from sin in the future. It is, after all, primarily, this resolution, too, which obtains absolution from sins actually committed." Samson Raphael Hirsch, *The Pentateuch, Vol. II, Exodus*, Translated by Isaac Levy, 2nd Edition (New York: Bloch Publishing Company, 1960), p. 550.

10. For a more extensive discussion of this topic see Henry W. Soltau, *The Holy Vessels and Furniture of the Tabernacle* (Grand Rapids: Kregel Publications, n.d.), p. 148. See also Roland deVaux, *Ancient Israel, Vol. II; Religious Institutions* (New York. Toronto: McGraw-Hill Book Company, 1965), pp. 418-420. See also H. H. Rowley, *Worship in Ancient Israel: Its Forms and Meaning, op. cit.*, pp. 128-129. Also Hans-Joachim Kraus, *Worship in Israel*, translated by Geoffrey Buswell (Oxford: Basil Blackwell, 1966), p. 121.

11. Roland deVaux, *Ancient Israel*, Vol. II; *Religious Institutions* (New York: McGraw-Hill Book Company, 1965), p. 420.

12. *Ibid.*

13. Chester K. Lehman, *Biblical Theology, Vol. I, Old Testament* (Scottdale: Herald Press, 1971), p. 154.

14. H. H. Rowley, *Worship in Ancient Israel: Its Forms and Meaning, op. cit.*, p. 120, 121.

15. Hans-Joachim Kraus, *Worship in Israel*, Translated by Geoffrey Buswell (Oxford: Basil Blackwell, 1966), p. 118.

16. Leviticus 7:30, 34; 8:27; 9:21; 10:14; 14:12, 24.

17. Leviticus 7:14, 32, 34; 10:14, 15; Numbers 6:20;15:19-21;18:8,11,19.

18. Olford bases his view on the work of John Kitto. See Stephen F. Olford, *The Tabernacle; Camping with God* (Neptune, New Jersey: Loizeaux Brothers, 1971), p. 100.

19. Strong says, "That it was shallow; raised but little from the ground may be inferred from its use; which was to wash the feet as well as the hands; that it was comparatively small may be inferred from the fact it was not intended for washing the entire person (vv. 19, 21)." Strong goes on to suggest its material, from the mirrors of the women, was very much like that which the Egyptian ladies were known to have used. James Strong, *The Tabernacle of Israel in the Desert* (Grand Rapids: Baker Book House, 1952), p. 19.

20. See Moshe Levine, *The Tabernacle: Its Structure and Utensils* (London. Jerusalem. New York: Published for the Soncino Press Limited, 1969) pp. 120, 121.

21. Gustave Friedrich Oehler *Theology of the Old Testament* (Grand Rapids: Zondervan Publishing House, n.d.), p. 256.

Chapter 3

1. A Jewish commentator interprets the metals differently: "Whereas copper represents an ignoble nature, one not yet refined, silver describes the stage of still requiring purification, but of being able and fit to be refined; gold is usually found pure, and unmixed, and also resists the strongest tests, is the picture of the purest, most sterling, moral nobility and of true, real permanence and constancy. As metals combine the highest degree of rimness and stability; under heat and hammer can be adapted to any desired form, but once they have received that form, retain it with a persistence that can only be destroyed by violence, they represent by these properties just those very characteristics that we should have towards our duty in general, and especially toward the will of God, as revealed to us by His Word." Samson Raphael Hirsch, *The Pentateuch, Vol. II, Exodus*, Translated by Isaac Levy, 2nd Edition (New York: Bloch Publishing Company, 1960), pp. 429, 430.

2. R. H. Mount, Jr., *The Law Prophesied* (Mansfield, Ohio: Mount Publications, 2nd Ed. 1963), p. 57.

3. Among writers taking this view are Cross, *op. cit.*, p. 62; Haran, *op. cit.*, p. 192, *The International Standard Bible Encyclopedia; The Interpreter's Dictionary of the Bible;* and *Encyclopedia Judaica.*

4. Levine says, "Both the length and breadth of the boards are indicated in the Torah. The Talmud (Shabbat 98B) adds the necessary information as to their thickness. The thickness of the boards was one cubit at the bottom narrowing towards the top to a finger's breadth; these are the words of Rabbi Judah. Rabbi Nehemiah says: "As they were one cubit thick at the bottom, so was their thickness at the top one cubit." The view

of Rabbi Nehemiah is accepted." Moshe Levine, *The Tabernacle; Its Structure and Utensils* (London. Jerusalem. New York: Published for the Soncino Press Limited, 1969), p. 22.

5. Josephus says they were square. Levine says the construction of the tabernacle was affected by Egyptian and Canaanite influence. Levine, *op. cit.*, pp. 43, 47. See also Cross, *op. cit.*, p. 61. Round pillars arose during the Greek and Roman periods. The model of the second temple (Herod's), which can be seen at the Holy Land hotel area near Jerusalem, has both square and round pillars which may symbolize the infiltration of the Greek and Roman world upon the Jewish community in the first century AD.

6. See Brown, Driver, and Briggs, *A Hebrew and English Lexicon of the Old Testament*, (Oxford: Clarendon Press, 1907), p. 1015.

7. Haran says, "At first sight it would seem that they [the woven pieces making up the bottom covering] are of the same mixture as the *paroketh*-veil woven according to the same *hoshev* workmanship with the figures of cherubim (Exodus 26:1; 36:8). Nevertheless, neither their composition nor outward appearance are actually identical with that of the *paroketh*. For it may be noted that, while in the ingredients of the *paroketh*, blue yarn is mentioned first and linen at the end, in these curtains, conversely, the linen is mentioned first and the three kinds of wool only afterward. Evidently this order of words which recurs punctiously in the two parallel descriptions alludes to the method by which this wool-linen mixture is to be constituted; i.e., in what proportions the different materials are to be woven together. The *paroketh* is to be made up, in the main, of the varieties of wool with the linen added to its mixture only at the end. The reverse order is to be taken in the lower curtains. It may be said that just as the *paroketh*-veil, the most important of the fabrics, corresponds to the articles of furniture in the inner sanctum, so the tabernacle curtains may be taken as corresponding, in the scale of gradations, to the outer sanctums's furniture." Menahem Haran, "The Priestly Image of the Tabernacle," *Hebrew Union College Annual*, Vol. XXXVI (1965), pp. 203, 204.

8. James A. Patch writes, "In the great sketches of uncultivated lands in the interior of Syria or Arabia, which probably have made the same aspect today as in Abraham's time, it is an easy matter to espy an encampment of roving Bedouin, 'a nation, that dwelleth without care . . . that have neither gates nor bars' (Jeremiah 49:31). The peaks of their black (cf. Cant 1:5) goats' hair tents stand out in contrast against the lighter colors of the soil. There seems to be little doubt about the antiquity of the Arab tent, and one can rightly believe that the dwelling places of Abraham, Sarah, Jacob, and their descendants were made of the same pattern and of the same materials. . . . The Arab tents (called *bait sha'r*, 'house of hair')

are made of strips of black goats' hair cloth, sewed together into one large piece." Article "tent," by James A. Patch, *The International Standard Bible Encyclopedia*, Vol. V (Grand Rapids: Wm. B. Eerdmans Publishing Co., 1939), p. 2947.

9. Despite many authors, including the highly respected James Strong, holding that the Tent *(ohel)* covering was separated from the tabernacle in an A-type appearance with ridge pole in the center, I am not yet convinced. For the flat-type view see Levine, *op. cit.*, pp. 51-67. My view is that the difference in Hebrew terms used for the first and second coverings speaks more directly to the kind of material used rather than the shape of the tabernacle.

10. For a more extended explanation of these views, see Levine, *op. cit.*, pp. 64-66.

11. M. R. Dehann, *The Tabernacle, House of Blood,* (Grand Rapids: Zondervan Publishing House, 1955), pp. 60, 61.

12. Frank M. Cross, Jr., "The Tabernacle," *The Biblical Archeologist*, Vol. X, No. 3 (September 1947), p. 62. Haran acknowledges Cross's view but does not fully commit himself either way. Haran, *op. cit.*, pp. 194, 204.

Chapter 4

1. Haran describes it as *roqem* workmanship. Levine disagrees with Haran and says cherubim were woven into it. But since the passages do not clarify it either way, I am inclined to follow Haran's view. Levine goes on to say, "Twenty-four threads of linen, and wool of various colors—blue, purple, scarlet—and threads of gold were used for the tapestry work. Each thread was twisted sixfold, so that the four different kinds, twined together, made up a thread of 24 strands." Moshe Levine, *The Tabernacle; Its Structure and Utensils* (London. Jerusalem. New York: Published for the Soncino Press Limited, 1969), p. 48.

2. James Strong says, "the mode of manufacture indicates that it was hollow, and Josephus affirms that this was the case." James Strong, *The Tabernacle of Israel in the Desert* (Grand Rapids: Baker Book House, 1952), p. 44.

3. *Ibid.*, p. 47.

4. J. H. Hertz, Ed., *The Pentatauch and Haftorahs*, Second Edition (London; Soncino Press, 5734-1973, 16th Impression), p. 339.

5. It should be noted this was a lampstand not a candlestick. It was a stand upon which lamps were placed, which is the meaning of the Hebrew and Greek terms used. Much later in history candles and candlesticks came into existence.

6. Wallace B. Nicholson, *The Hebrew Sanctuary* (Grand Rapids: Baker Book House, 1951), p. 41.

7. This is the view set forth by Henry W. Soltau, *The Holy Vessels and Furniture of the Tabernacle* (Grand Rapids: Kregel Publications reprint), pp. 60, 61.

8. See Strong, *op. cit.*, p. 42. See also Levine, *op. cit.*, pp. 98-101.

9. Quoted by Alfred Edersheim, *The Temple: Its Ministry and Services* (Grand Rapids: Wm. B. Eerdmans Publishing Company, 1969 reprint), pp. 185, 186.

10. Levine, *op. cit.*, p. 92.

11. Strong, *op. cit.*, p. 60.

12. James F. Spink, *Types and Shadows of Christ in the Tabernacle* (New York: Loizeaux Brothers, 1946), pp. 79, 80.

13. David Little, *The Tabernacle in the Wilderness* (New York: Loizeaux Brothers, 3rd Printing, 1957), pp. 37, 38.

14. *Ibid.*, p. 38.

15. Hertz says, "The rabbis explained that the four letters of the Hebrew word for incense, קטרת , stood for: קדושה , holiness; טהרה, purity; רחמים,pity: and תקוה, hope—a wonderful summary of the prerequisites of prayer and of its spiritual results in the lives of men." Hertz. *op. cit*, p. 349.

Chapter 5

1. Moshe Levine, *The Tabernacle; Its Structure and Utensils* (London, Jerusalem. New York: Published for the Soncinio Press Limited, 1969), p. 38.

2. Alfred Edersheim, *The Life and Times of Jesus the Messiah*, Vol. II (New York: Longmans, Green, and Col, 1906), p. 611.

3. The most frequently used term is ark of the covenant. However, other terms are used such as "ark of God" (1 Samuel 3:3), "The ark of the Lord" (Joshua 4:11), or in some cases simply "the ark" (Exodus 25:14).

4. Morgenstern thinks it may have been a red leather tent shrine *(qubbah)* transported by camel back, but his view is rejected in light of contemporary scholarship reflected in Newman's study. "It is unlikely that the ark was a tent, as has been suggested. . . . But the general picture of a portable shrine made of acacia wood in the shape of a chest is quite consonant with all the early passages in the Old Testament which pertain to the ark." Murray Lee Newman, Jr., *The People of the Covenant* (London: The Carey Kingsgate Press Limited, 1965), pp. 55, 58.

5. We need not be alarmed about Deuteronomy 31:26 which says the law was beside the ark of the covenant instead of in it. At either place it witnessed to the fact of the close tie between the law and God along with the law's close tie to the mercy seat and the covenant.

6. Tereance Erling Fretheim, *The Cultic Use of the Ark of the Covenant in the Monarchial Period* (Unpublished ThD dissertation,

Princeton Theological Seminary, 1967, Copyright, 1968), p. 247.

7. See, for example, Psalm 9:12; 15:1; 24:7-10; 44:10; 47:6; 63:3; 68:2; 78:61; 96:6; 99:5; 101:2; 132.

8. Fretheim says, "The relationship of Yahweh to the ark was so close that to be 'before the ark' was to be 'before Jehovah.' When the ark came into the Israelite camp, the narrator has the Philistines say: '(A) God has come into the camp.' The processions of the ark are referred to as the processions of God Himself. The ark is addressed as if Yahweh Himself was being addressed. On the other hand, passages in these same contexts show that Yahweh was conceived to be present apart from the ark. Taken together these references suggest that it is best to adopt the idea of A. R. Johnson that the ark is understood as an 'extension' of the personality of Yahweh. . . . The ark makes God's presence real without tying Him down to a particular locality." Fretheim, *op. cit.*, pp. 220, 221.

9. Newman, *op. cit.*, p. 61.

10. Fretheim, *op. cit.*, p. 252.

11. W. G. Moorehead, *Studies in the Mosaic Institutions* (Dayton, Ohio: United Brethren Publishing House, 1909), p. 85. Note the Greek prepositions used in John 14:16, 17 to describe God's presence in the Holy Spirit.

12. *Ibid.*, p. 81.

13. B. F. Westcott, *The Epistle to the Hebrews* (Grand Rapids: Wm. B. Eerdmans Publishing Company, N.d.), p. 229.

14. The term used for this scapegoat is *azazel* which, according to Hertz, "is the ancient technical term for the entire removal of the sin and guilt of the community, that was symbolized by the sending away of the goat into the wilderness. In the *Talmud, azazel* was translated by 'steep mountain,' and was applied to the rock in the wilderness from which in later times the animal was hurled." J. H. Hertz, Editor, *The Pentateuch and Haftorahs* (London: Soncino Press, Second Edition, Sixteenth Impression, 5734-1973), p. 481.

15. Quoted from *The Mishnah*, trans. by Herbert Danby (Oxford: Clarendon Press, 1933) by C. K. Barrett, *The New Testament Background: Selected Documents* (New York: Harper & Row, Publishers, 1961) pp. 159-162.

16. Newman, *op. cit.*, p. 58.

17. There is considerable misunderstanding regarding the shape of cherubim on the ark of the covenant, the veil, and the *mishkan* covering over the top of the tabernacle. Cherubim are described differently in each of the following passages: Genesis 3:24; Exodus 25:18-20; Exodus 37:7-9; Isaiah 6:2; Ezekiel 10. In medieval art human beings were painted with wings between AD 1100-1200. This is the common conception of cherubim today. However, research shows they were animals with wings.

Note the picture and description of a cherub found by archeologists, dated the 9th century BC in the revised edition of the *Jewish Encyclopedia.* DeVaux says, "The cherubim were winged animals with human heads, like the winged sphinxes of Syro-Phoenician iconography." Roland deVaux, *Ancient Israel, Vol. II. Religious Institutions* (New York: McGraw-Hill Book Company, 1965), p. 319.

18. A few scholars reject the idea that the ark of the covenant and the cherubim meant God's rule and reign. For example, Martin H. Woudstra turns this view aside. See *The Ark of the Covenant from Conquest to Kingship* (Philadelphia: Presbyterian and Reformed Publishing Company, 1965). Scriptural references that refer to the ark of the covenant as the throne of God are: Numbers 10:35, 36; 1 Samuel 4:4; 2 Samuel 6:2; 2 Kings 19:14, 15; Jeremiah 3:16, 17; Ezekiel 43:7. Contemporary scholars who hold to the position that the reign of God is indicated by the ark of the covenant and the cherubim include Clements, Newman, Kraus, Lind, and Eichrodt.

Chapter 6

1. As quoted by C. S. Slemming, *These Are the Garments* (Henry E. Walter LTD, Worthing: 26 Grafton Road and London: Revised Edition, 1955), p. 10.

2. See Footnote 19 in F. F. Bruce, *The Epistle to the Hebrews* (Grand Rapids: Wm. B. Eerdmans Publishing Co., 1964), p. 92.

3. Samson Raphad Hirsch, *The Pentateuch, Vol. II, Exodus;* Translated by Issac Levy, 2nd Edition (New York: Bloch Publishing Company, 1960), p. 531.

4. Slemming, *op. cit.*, p. 166.

5. Menahem Haran, "The Priestly Image of the Tabernacle," *Hebrew Union College Annual*, Vol. XXXVI (1965), p. 210.

6. Moshe Levine, *The Tabernacle; Its Structure and Utensils* (London. Jerusalem. New York: Published for Soncino Press Limited, 1969) pp. 124, 128.

7. The number of bells and pomegranates is not given in the biblical text. Hirsch believes there were 72 bells and 72 pomegranates. Haran indicates that there is no evidence in the text regarding the number of each. Levine, however, argues for a total of 72 bells and pomegranates. The present writer feels the best answer is that we do not know how many there were, but perhaps the answer with the least amount of problems is Levine's view.

8. Haran, *op. cit.*, pp. 208, 209.

9. W. G. Moorehead, *Studies in the Mosaic Institutions* (Dayton: United Brethren Publishing House, 1909), p. 96.

10. See E. L. Gilmore, "Which Were the Original Twelve Gemstones

of the Biblical Breastplace?" *Lapidary Journal*, Vol. XIV, No. 3 (August, 1960), pp. 242ff. The listing in English Bibles does not follow the order in the Hebrew text. We do not know if the stones listed imply the order of tribes according to birth, as was the case with the listing on the shoulders of the high priest, or if the order implied is that of the arrangement of the tribes in the encampment.

11. Levine says, "Between the plate and the mitre was a gap, providing space for the tephillin (Phylacteries) worn on top of the forehead where the hair begins to grow." Levine, *op. cit.*, p. 140.

Chapter 7

1. In Numbers 4 the age of service is between 30 and 50 years. But in Numbers 8:24, 25 the beginning age of service is 25 years. Later in Israel's history the Levites were given greater tasks including priestly functions. See Jacob Milgrom, "Studies in the Temple Scroll," *Journal of Biblical Literature*, Vol. 97, No. 4 (December 1978), pp. 501-523.

2. They covered the ark of the covenant without seeing it. Perhaps since God's presence had already moved from the ark and went ahead of the line or march, there was no problem with priests seeing the ark. Some hold the view that the priests stood with their faces looking eastward and reached up behind their backs and unhooked the veil and then, stepping backward, laid the veil over the ark. Another possibility is that they held the veil above their heads and walked westward until the veil covered the ark of the covenant.

3. Newman says, "If there are two early traditions concerning the covenant at Sinai, it is noteworthy that there are also early traditions concerning two important shrines at Sinai. The ark of the covenant and the tent of meeting both appear for the first time at Sinai. It seems probable that the E covenant legend is to be associated with the ark and the J legend with the tent." Murray Lee Newman, Jr., *The People of the Covenant* (London: The Carey Kingsgate Press Limited, 1962), p. 55. Newman associated Numbers 10:33-36 with the ark saying it is the earliest tradition related to the ark at Mt. Sinai. He associated Exodus 33:7-11; Numbers 11:16, 17; 24-30; 12 and Deuteronomy 31:14, 15 with the tent of meeting.

4. Hans Joachim Kraus, *Worship in Israel;* translated by Geoffrey Buswell (Oxford: Basil Blackwell, 1966), p. 127. Terrence Erling Fretheim, *The Cultic Use of the Ark of the Covenant in the Monarchial Period* (Unpublished ThD dissertation, Princeton Theological Seminary, 1967, Copyright 1968), pp. 99, 100. Newman, *op. cit.*, pp. 67, 68.

5. Frank M. Cross, Jr., "The Tabernacle," *The Biblical Archeologist*, Vol. X, No. 3 (September 1947), p. 59.

6. Kraus, *op. cit.*, p. 127.

7. Roland deVaux, *Ancient Israel; Vol. II, Religious Institutions* (New York: McGraw-Hill Book Company, 1965), p. 298.

8. Levine says, "According to tradition, the tabernacle was erected on the first day of Nissan, in the year of Creation 2449, that is almost 3,300 years ago." Moshe Levine, *The Tabernacle, Its Structure and Utensils* (London. Jerusalem. New York: Published for the Soncino Press Limited, 1969), p. 14.

9. *Ibid.*

10. Second Samuel 6:17. Here the word "tent" obviously means tabernacle and is used interchangeably with tabernacle. In 1 Samuel 3:3, Samuel was lying down in the "temple" before the Lord. Obviously, since the first temple was not built until several years later, Samuel laid in the tabernacle. For a recent study on the biblical narrative covering these events (1 Samuel 4—6; 2 Samuel 6), see Anthony F. Campbell, "Yahweh and the Ark: A Case Study in Narrative," *Journal of Biblical Literature*, Vol. 98, No. 1 (March 1979), pp. 31-43. Campbell begins this article by saying, "Attention has been focused on the Ark Narrative(s) with a vengence, these last five years. Not in the fifty years of its history among the hypotheses of biblical scholarship has it received such concentrated consideration as in three recent monographs, by Schicklberger, Campbell—the present writer—and Miller and Roberts."

11. James Strong, *The Tabernacle of Israel in the Desert* (Grand Rapids: Baker Book House, 1952), p. 10.

12. Josephus, *Wars* V, v, 5. See, for example, 2 Maccabees 2:4-5; 2 Baruch 6:7-10; 2 Esdras 10:22. DeVaux reports that one speculative view said that Jeremiah had hidden the ark, the tent, and the incense altar in a cave on Mt. Nebo. DeVaux, *op. cit.*, p. 299.

13. Quoted in C. K. Barrett, *The New Testament Background; Selected Documents* (New York: Harper & Row, Publishers, 1961), p. 160.

Chapter 8

1. Menahem Haran, "The Priestly Image of the Tabernacle," *Hebrew Union College Annual*, Vol. XXXVI (1965), p. 202. Haran's article is most helpful in identifying three kinds of workmanship in the fabrics of the tabernacle.

2. The Greek term skene (σκηνή) is the LXX translation of mishkan (משכן). John 1:14, therefore, means God tabernacled among us in Jesus Christ.

3. The author of Hebrews is not merely borrowing Platonic ideas when he talks about the heavenly sanctuary. Rather, he is picking up a threefold tie between Old Testament forms, the New Testament realization, and the heavenly reality. The author of Hebrews has a dualistic eschatology in which the future fullness of the kingdom is breaking into the

present age. He applies that dualism to the Old Testament cult and tabernacle. C. K. Barrett says, "The heavenly tabernacle in Hebrews is not the product of Platonic idealism but the eschatological temple of apocalyptic Judaism, the temple which is in heaven primarily in order that it may be manifested on earth." Quoted by George Eldon Ladd, *A Theology of the New Testament* (Grand Rapids: Wm. B. Eerdmans Publishing Company, 1974), p. 576.

4. The Greek term *hilastarion* from which our English word expiation comes is used by the LXX translators for the Hebrew term *Kapporeth*, the term for mercy seat at the ark of the covenant. Thus, Paul declares Christ and His cross are the means by which a holy God and sinful man are reconciled. For at that cross sin is properly dealt with and removed thereby making reconciliation a reality.

5. In 1 Enoch 90 the Maccabees are symbolized as "horned lambs." In the Testament of Joseph a lamb destroys the enemies of Israel (19:8). And in 1 Enoch 90:37 the military leader is the "white bull with large horns."

Chapter 9

1. Harold S. Bender, *These Are My People* (Scottdale: Herald Press, 1962), pp. 18, 19.

2. Robert Friedmann says, "In Catholicism the believer is offered, as the only effective way to God and salvation, an intermediary, the institutional church with its reservoir of divine grace, and with its ordained priests who dispense the sacraments. In Protestantism, this intermediary was radically done away with. Each individual believer stands in direct, unmediated relationship to his God seeking and finding redemption by faith to the extent that he is able to have such a redeeming faith. In Anabaptism, finally, the answer is a combination of a vertical with a horizontal relationship. Here the thesis is accepted that *man cannot come to God except together with his brother*. Robert Friedmann, *The Theology of Anabaptism* (Scottdale: Herald Press, 1973), pp. 80, 81.

3. Romans 10:9, 10; 1 Corinthians 12:3; Philippians 2:6-11.

4. 1 Corinthians 15:20-28; Ephesians 1:19-23; Colossians 1:15-20; 2:15. See also 1 Peter 3:22.

5. Oscar Cullman uses this phrase to describe his view of eschatology. George E. Ladd has a similar interpretation of the kingdom of God.

Chapter 10

1. Chester K. Lehman, *Biblical Theology*, Vol. I (Scottdale: Herald Press, 1971), p. 147.

Appendix I

1. Roland de Vaux, *Ancient Israel; Its Life and Institutions*, translated

by John McHugh (New York. Toronto. London: McGraw-Hill Book Company, Inc., 1961), pp. 274-275. (For information on the extent of Israel's borrowing from the Canaanites, see Hans-Joachim Kraus, *Worship in Israel*, translated by Geoffrey Buswell (Oxford: Basel Blackwell, 1966), pp. 36, 112, 113. See also R. E. Clements, *God and Temple* (Philadelphia: Fortress Press, 1965), pp. 2-4, 17.

2. John Bright, *A History of Israel* (Philadelphia: The Westminster Press, 1959), p. 149.

3. H. H. Rowley, *From Moses to Qumran* (New York: Association Press, 1963), p. 68.

4. Jackson says, "With the revival of interest in biblical theology has come a renewed concern for the history of religious institutions. Indeed, one could say that investigation into the worship of the people of Israel has become a major area of inquiry. The question of the relationship between cult and history is in the very forefront of Old Testament discussion today." Jared Jud Jackson, *The Ark Narratives; an Historical, Textual and Form-Critical Study of I Samuel 4-6 and II Samuel 6* (New York: Unpublished ThD dissertation, Union Theological Seminary, 1962), p. vi.

An exhaustive bibliography cannot be given here. But the following recent books and articles clearly show the new interest in the subject:

Frank M. Cross, Jr., "The Tabernacle," *The Biblical Archeologist*, Vol. X, No. 3 (September 1947), pp. 45 ff.

D. W. Gooding, *The Account of the Tabernacle* (Cambridge: The University Press, 1959).

Menahem Haran, "The Nature of the 'Ohel Mo'ed' in Pentateuchal Sources," *Journal of Semetic Studies*, Vol. V (1960), pp. 60-65.

Roland de Vaux, *Ancient Israel; Its Life and Institutions*, translated by John McHugh (New York. Toronto. London: McGraw-Hill Book Company, Inc., 1961).

Murray Lee Newman, Jr., *The People of the Covenant* (London: The Carey Kingsgate Press Limited, 1962).

H. H. Rowley, *From Moses to Qumran* (New York: Association Press, 1963). See the chapter entitled "The Meaning of Sacrifice in the Old Testament."

Menahem Haran, "The Priestly Image of the Tabernacle," *Hebrew Union College Annual*, Vol. XXXVI, (1965), pp. 191-226.

R. E. Clements, *God and Temple* (Philadelphia: Fortress Press, 1965).

Hans-Joachim Kraus, *Worship in Israel*, translated by Geoffrey Buswell (Oxford: Basel Blackwell, 1966).

H. H. Rowley, *Worship in Ancient Israel; Its Forms and Meaning* (Philadelphia: Fortress Press, 1967).

Moshe Levine, *The Tabernacle: Its Structure and Utensils* (London.

Jerusalem. New York: Soncino Press, Limited, 1969).

In addition to these recent articles and books are two unpublished doctoral dissertations. Jackson's, listed above, and Terrence Erling Fretheim, *The Cultic Use of the Ark of the Covenant in the Monarchial Period* (unpublished ThD dissertation, Princeton Theological Seminary, 1968).

5. Newman believes both the ark of the covenant and tent of meeting appear for the first time at Sinai and that the discussion of the ark is carried by the E document and the tent of meeting by the J document. He associates Numbers 10:33-36 with the ark saying it is the earliest tradition related to the ark at Mt. Sinai. He associates Exodus 33:7-11; Numbers 11:16, 17; 24-30; 12; and Deuteronomy 31:14, 15 with the tent of meeting. For a detailed discussion, see Murray Lee Newman, Jr., *The People of the Covenant* (London: The Carey Kingsgate Press, Limited, 1962), pp. 39-71.

6. Hans-Joachim Kraus, *Worship in Israel*, translated by Geoffrey Buswell (Oxford: Basel Blackwell, 1966), p. 127. See also Terrence Erling Fretheim, *The Cultic Use of the Ark of the Covenant in the Monarchial Period* (unpublished ThD dissertation, Princeton Theological Seminary, 1968), pp. 70-77.

7. Cross says, "Often the priestly scribes placed their ancient sources in the wrong context, but the day when their work could be universally rejected as "pious fraud" has passed. . . . While the J stratum strongly emphasized the covenant at Sinai, and E describes both the revelation of Yahweh's name and the formation of the covenant in the desert, it is particularly the tabernacle traditions which maintain that Yahweh was first worshiped in the desert, and that the cultic institutions and the formation of the state . . . find their origin under Moses in the desert." Frank M. Cross, Jr., "The Tabernacle," *The Biblical Archeologist*, Vol. X, No. 3 (September 1947), p. 52. See also Kraus, *op. cit.*, pp. 19, 20.

8. Bernhard W. Anderson, *Understanding the Old Testament*, Third Edition (Englewood Cliffs, N.J.: Prentice-Hall, Inc., 1975), p. 80. See page 162 for a similar statement.

9. Kraus, *op. cit.*, p. 127. Cross, *op. cit.*, p. 50. Frank Cross says, "The Ark has always been associated with a tent shrine, wherever it wandered, wherever the central sanctuary was established." Frank M. Cross, *Canaanite Myth and Hebrew Epic; Essays in the History of the Religion of Israel* (Cambridge: Harvard University Press, 1973), p. 242.

10. For a more extensive discussion of this term, see the following: Chester K. Lehman, *Biblical Theology*, Vol. I (Scottdale: Herald Press, 1971), p. 138. Walter Eichrodt, *Theology of the Old Testament*, Vol. I, translated by J. A. Baker (Philadelphia: The Westminster Press, 1961), p. 110. Julian Morgenstern, *The Ark, The Ephod and The "Tent of Meeting"* (Cincinnati: The Hebrew Union College Press, 1945), p. 132.

11. *'Ohel* is a masculine noun which occurs 360 times in the Hebrew Old Testament. It is translated *tabernacle* or its equivalent 218 times and 137 times it is rendered *tent.* Only three times is it translated dwelling and once it is rendered *covering.* With only minor deviations, the Septuagint translators used the Greek term *skana* to convey its meaning.

12. For a detailed analysis of the differences in the Septuagint translation of these narratives and their linguistic differences, see D. W. Gooding, *The Account of the Tabernacle* (Cambridge: The University Press, 1959).

13. *Mishkan* occurs approximately 140 times in the Old Testament. It is translated *tabernacle* except for 14 times when it is rendered *dwelling* or *dwelling place* and five times *habitation.* Its predominant translation in the LXX is *skana.*

14. F. Brown, S. R. Driver, and C. A. Briggs, *A Hebrew and English Lexicon of the Old Testament* (Oxford: Clarendon Press, 1907), pp. 1014, 1015. For further elaboration of this idea, see R. E. Clements, *God and Temple* (Philadelphia: Fortress Press, 1965), p. 116. See also Terrence Erling Fretheim *The Cultic Use of the Ark of the Covenant in the Monarchial Period* (Unpublished ThD dissertation, Princeton Theological Seminary, 1968), pp. 76, 77.

15. See Gerhard Kittel, *Theological Dictionary of the New Testament,* Vol. VIII, translated by Geoffrey Bromily (Grand Rapids: William B. Eerdmans Publishing Co., 1971) p. 371.

16. Bernard Ramm, *Protestant Biblical Interpretation* (Boston: W. A. Wilde Company, 1950), p. 24.

17. Quoted by Wallace B. Nicholson, *The Hebrew Sanctuary* (Grand Rapids: Baker Book House, 1951), p. 8. In a footnote, James Strong says, "Much that has been given by former writers as symbol on this subject is merely metaphor or figure of speech instead of representation by object. The symbolism of the tabernacle, as developed by Josephus and Philo, is purely cosmical... Such whims can neither be proved or disproved; the competent objection to this is their inadequacy and their triviality." James Strong, *The Tabernacle of Israel in The Desert* (Grand Rapids: Baker Book House, 1952), p. 71.

18. Nicholson, *op. cit.,* pp. 7, 8.

BIBLIOGRAPHY

I. Reference Works

Brown, F., S. R. Driver, and C. A. Briggs, *A Hebrew and English Lexicon of the Old Testament* (Oxford: Clarendon Press, 1907).

Buttrick, George A., Ed., *The Interpreter's Dictionary of the Bible* (New York, Nashville: Abingdon Press, 1962).

Davis, John P., and Henry Snyder Gehman, *The Westminster Dictionary of the Bible* (Philadelphia: Westminster Press, Revised Edition, 1944).

Hastings, James, Ed., *Dictionary of the Bible*, Revised Edition by Frederick C. Grant and H. H. Rowley (New York: Scribner's, 1963).

Hatch, Edwin, and Henry A. Redpath, *A Concordance to the Septuagint*, Vol. II (Graz-Austria: Akademische Druck-U. Verlagsanstalt, 1897).

Hertz, J. H., Ed., *The Pentateuch and Haftorahs*, 2nd Edition (London: Soncino Press, 5734-1973, 16th Impression).

Hirsch, Samson Raphael, *The Pentateuch, Vol. II, Exodus*, Translated by Isaac Levy, 2nd. Edition (New York: Bloch Publishing Company, 1960).

Jackson, Samuel Macauley, Ed. in Chief, *The New Schaff-Herzog Encyclopedia of Religious Knowledge*, Vol. XI (New York. London: Funk and Wagnalls, 1911).

Keil, C. F., and F. Delitzsch, *Biblical Commentary on the Old*

*Testament,*Translated by James Martin (Grand Rapids: Eerdmans, n. d.).

Kittel, Gerhard, Ed., *Theological Dictionary of the New Testament,* Vol. VIII (Grand Rapids: Eerdmans, 1971).

Orr, James, Gen. Ed., *The International Standard Bible Encyclopedia* (Grand Rapids: Eerdmans, 1939).

Roth, Cecil, Geoffrey Wigoder, Editors in Chief, *Encyclopedia Judaica,* Vol. XV (Jerusalem: Keter Publishing House, Ltd., 1971, and New York: Macmillan, 1972).

Singer, Isidore, Man. Ed., *The Jewish Encyclopedia,* Vol. XI (New York. London: Funk and Wagnalls, 1905).

Tenny, Merrill C., Gen. Ed., *The Zondervan Pictorial Bible Dictionary* (Grand Rapids: Zondervan, 1967).

Unger, Merrill F., *Unger's Bible Dictionary* (Chicago: Moody Press, 1957).

II. Books

Anderson, Bernhard W., *Understanding the Old Testament* (Englewood Cliffs, N. J.: Prentice-Hall, Inc., 1957).

Atwater, Edward E., *History and Significance of the Sacred Tabernacle* (New York: Dodd and Mead, Publishers, 1875).

Baxter, W. L. *Sanctuary and Sacrifice, A Reply to Wellhausen* (London: Eyre and Spottiswoode, 1896).

Bright, John, *A History of Israel* (Philadelphia: The Westminster Press, 1959).

__________ *The Kingdom of God* (New York. Nashville: Abingdon Press, 1953).

Brown, William, *The Tabernacle, Its Priests and Services* (Edinburgh: William Oliphant & Co., 1872).

Caldecott, *The Tabernacle; Its History and Structure* (Philadelphia: The Union Press, 1904).

Chambers, Laurence T., *Tabernacle Studies* (Grand Rapids: Zondervan Publishing House, 1958).

Clements, R. E., *God and Temple* (Philadelphia: Fortress Press, 1965).

Corbin, Bruce, *The Tabernacle in the Wilderness* (Enid, Oklahoma: Truth Publishing Company, n. d.).

de Charms, George, *The Tabernacle of Israel* (New York: Pageant Press International Corp., 1969).

De Haan, M. R., *The Tabernacle* (Grand Rapids: Zondervan Publishing House, 1955).

de Vaux, Roland, *Ancient Israel* (New York: McGraw-Hill Book Company, 1965).

Dilworth, John, *Pictorial Description of the Tabernacle in the Wilderness* (London: Sunday School Union, 56, Old Bailey, E. C., 1878).

Dolman, D. H. *Simple Talks on the Tabernacle* (Grand Rapids: Zondervan Publishing House, 1941).

Fuller, Charles E., *The Tabernacle in the Wilderness* (Westwood, N.J.: Fleming H. Revell Company, 1955).

Gooding, D. W., *The Account of the Tabernacle* (Cambridge: The University Press, 1959).

Habershon, Ada R., *Outline Studies of the Tabernacle* (London: Morgan and Scott, n. d.).

Hains, Edmont, *The Tabernacle* (Grand Rapids: Zondervan Publishing House, 1950).

Haldeman, I. M., *The Tabernacle Priesthood and Offerings* (New York: Fleming H. Revell Company, 1925)

Hicks, B. R., *Precious Gem in the Tabernacle* (Mexican Inland Society, 1961).

Ironside, H. A., *Lectures on the Levitical Offerings* (New York: Loizeaux Brothers, Inc., 1929).

Jukes, Andrew, *The Law of the Offerings* (London: The Lamp Press LtD, 1954).

Junkin, George, *The Tabernacle; Of the Gospel According to Moses* (Philadelphia: Presbyterian Board of Publication, 1865).

Kiene, Paul F., *The Tabernacle of God in the Wilderness of Sinai*, Translated by John S. Crandall (Grand Rapids: Zondervan Publishing House, 1977).

Kraus, Hans-Joachim, *Worship in Israel*, Translated by Geoffrey

Buswell (Oxford: Basil Blackwell, 1966).

Lehman, Chester K., *Biblical Theology*, Vol. I (Scottdale: Herald Press, 1971).

Levine, Moshe, *The Tabernacle; Its Structure and Utensils* (London. Jerusalem. New York: Published for the Soncino Press Limited, 1969).

Lewis, G. Wilton, *The Tabernacle of the Testimony from the Book of Exodus* (Cincinnati: The Standard Publishing Company, 1925).

Lind, Millard C., *Biblical Foundations for Christian Worship* (Scottdale: Herald Press, 1973).

Little, David, *The Tabernacle in the Wilderness* (New York: Loizeaux Brothers, Publishers, 3rd. Printing, Oct. 1957).

Maxfield, Helen Z., *The Tabernacle* (Grand Rapids: Zondervan Publishing House, 1950).

McCord, Iris Ikeler, *The Tabernacle; Its God-Appointed Structure and Service* (Chicago: Moody Press, 1927).

Moorehead, W. G., *Studies in the Mosaic Institutions* (Dayton: United Brethren Publishing House, 1909).

Morgenstern, Julian, *The Ark, the Ephod, and the "Tent of Meeting"* (Cincinnati: The Hebrew Union College Press, 1945).

Mount, R. H., Jr., *The Law Prophesied* (Mansfield, Ohio: Mount Publications, 2nd, ed., 1963).

Newberry, Thomas, *The Tabernacle and the Temple* (London: Hodder and Stoughton, 1887).

Newton, Benjamin Wills, *Thoughts on Parts of the Book of Leviticus* (London: The Sovereign Grace Advent Testimony, Sec. George H. Fromow, 9 Milnthorpe Road, Chiswick, W. 4, 1857, Second Ed.).

Newton, Richard, *The Jewish Tabernacle and Its Furniture in Their Typical Teachings* (New York: Robert Carter & Brothers, 1874).

Newman, Murray Lee, Jr., *The People of the Covenant* (London: The Carey Kingsgate Press Limited, 1962).

Nicholson, Wallace B., *The Hebrew Sanctuary* (Grand Rapids: Baker Book House, 1951).

Noth, Martin, *The History of Israel,* Translated by Stanley Godman, 2nd Edition (London: Adam & Charles Black, 1958).

Oehler, Gustave Friedrich, *Theology of the Old Testament,* Revised translation by George E. Day (Grand Rapids: Zondervan Publishing House, n. d.).

Olford, Stephen F., *The Tabernacle: Camping with God* (Neptune, New Jersey: Loizeaux Brothers, 1971).

Otto, John, *The Tabernacle and Its Furniture* (London: Benjamin L. Green, 62, Paternoster Row, 1849).

Pollock, Algernon J., *The Tabernacle's Typical Teaching* (London: Paternoster Row, n. d.).

Pont, Charles E., *Tabernacle Alphabet* (New York: Loizeaux Brothers, 1946).

Rhind, W. G., *The Tabernacle in the Wilderness; the Shadow of Heavenly Things* (London: Samuel Bagster and Sons, Paternoster Row, 1845, Fourth Edition).

Ridout, S., *Lectures on the Tabernacle* (New York: Loizeaux Brothers, 1945).

Ritchie, John, *The Tabernacle in the Wilderness* (Kilmarnock, Briton: John Ritchie LtD, n.d.)

Rowley, H. H., *From Moses to Qumran* (New York: Association Press, 1963).

———— *Worship in Ancient Israel: Its Forms and Meaning* (Philadelphia: Fortress Press, 1967).

Russell, Charles T., *Tabernacle Shadows of the Better Sacrifices* (Philadelphia: Paul S. L. Johnson, 1937).

Slemming, C. W., *These Are the Garments* (Published by Henry E. Walter LtD, Worthing: 26 Grafton Road and London, Revised Edition, 1956).

Soltau, Henry W., *The Holy Vessels and Furniture of the Tabernacle* (Grand Rapids: Kregel Publications, Reprint of the 1851 edition by Yapp and Hawkins, London, n.d.).

Spink, James F., *Types and Shadows of Christ in the Tabernacle* (New York, Loizeaux Brothers, 1946).

Strong, James, *The Tabernacle of Israel in the Desert* (Grand

Rapids: Baker Book House, 1952).

von Rod, Gerhard, *Old Testament Theology,* Vol. I. Translated by D. M. G. Stalker (New York. Evanston: Harper & Row, Publishers, 1962).

Vos, Geerhardus, *Biblical Theology, Old and New Testaments* (Grand Rapids: Wm. B. Eerdmans Publishing Company, 1959).

Woudstra, Marten H., *The Ark of the Covenant from Conquest to Kingship* (Philadelphia: Presbyterian and Reformed Publishing Company, 1965).

III. Articles and Periodicals

Cross, Frank M., Jr., "The Tabernacle," *The Biblical Archeologist,* Vol. X, No. 3 [Sept. 1947].

Haran, Menahem, "The Nature of the ''Ohel Mo'ed' in Pentateuchal Sources," *Journal of Semitic Studies,* Vol. V., (1960), pp. 50-65.

__________"The Preistly Image of the Tabernacle," *Hebrew Union College Annual,* Vol. XXXVI (1965), pp. 191-226.

Rabe, Virgil W., "The Identity of the Priestly Tabernacle," *Journal of Near Eastern Studies,* Vol. XXV, (1966), pp. 132-134.

IV. Unpublished Works

Fretheim, Terrence Erling, *The Cultic Use of the Ark of the Covenant in the Monarchial Period* (Unpublished ThD dissertation, Princeton Theological Seminary, 1967, Copyright 1968).

Jackson, Jared Judd, *The Ark Narratives; An Historical, Textual, and Form-Critical Study of I Samuel 4-6 and II Samuel 6* (New York: Unpublished ThD dissertation, Union Theological Seminary, 1962).

SCRIPTURE INDEX

OLD TESTAMENT

Leviticus

NEW TESTAMENT

Paul M. Zehr has lectured on the Old Testament tabernacle for nearly ten years, first at a reproduction of the tabernacle in St. Petersburg, Florida. Later he directed the building of a tabernacle reproduction in Lancaster, Pennsylvania, and taught others to lecture on it.

Born and reared at Croghan, New York, Zehr was educated at Eastern Mennonite College, Eastern Mennonite Seminary, Princeton Theological Seminary, and The Eastern Baptist Theological Seminary.

He was ordained to the ministry in Sarasota, Florida, and served as pastor of the First Mennonite Church in St. Petersburg from 1965 to 1973. From 1973 to 1987 he pastored the hearing group of the First Deaf Mennonite Church in Lancaster, Pennsylvania. In 1980 he was ordained bishop of the Mellinger District of Lancaster Mennonite Conference.

The author served the Lancaster Conference of the Mennonite

Church as secretary of its coordinating council and director of pastoral training.

Zehr s leadership in the Mennonite Church includes eight years of service on the General Board. He has also been moderator of the Region V Assembly of the Mennonite Church and more recently vice-president of the Mennonite Board of Education.

His writings include curriculum materials for youth and adults, articles, and a booklet, *Biblical Criticism in the Life of the Church* (Herald Press, 1986).

Paul and his wife, Mary Martin Zehr, have four children—two daughters (Karen and Marcia) and two sons (Timothy and Daniel).